MW01268190

AFRICA AND CHILDREN

AFRICA AND CHILDREN

J. Ninsel Warner

J. Ninsel Warner, Sr.

Brooklyn Center, MN

Cover design by Tamika L. Hayden, TLH Designs
Chicago, IL.

Cover Photo by Jack Horst, Naaldwijk, Netherlands
http://www.sxc.hu/profile/djinas

Book design by Kingdom Living Publishing
Fort Washington, MD

Printed in the United States of America.

ISBN 978-0-615-48050-3

Acknowledgment

We would like to register our gratitude to all our friends and relatives for the moral support given us during the entire exercise. Special word of appreciation also goes to my sister Annie Serena Warner-Epps, who lives in Durham, NC, and my friend Morris Gweh of Los Angeles, CA, for all the financial arrangements concluded to assist in publishing this work.

Of equal importance, we are indebted to Professor Andrew Jolly of Stephens College, Missouri, under whom this work was written as a short story in his Creative Writing class at the University of Liberia in Monrovia. Professor Jolly served as a Fulbright Fellow at the University of Liberia while we were students. The personal interest which Professor Jolly manifested in us made a difference in what we are today.

The incessant efforts and encouragement of my wife, Mary Musu-Warner, to a larger degree, buttressed our strength and the will to publish this work; and for which we are very grateful.

Table of Content

Foreword

Liberia (a small West African country, the size of Ohio) was founded by freed slaves from the United States of America in 1847. Much was expected from the settlers since, indeed, they returned to their motherland in search of freedom, justice, equality and equal opportunity for all. The natives were expected to receive their brothers and sisters wholeheartedly, but this was not the case from the onset. There were several wars between the founders and the natives due to lack of complete understanding between the two groups.

After toiling in America for over 200 years, the settlers had lost almost all their African identities, including African languages. The natives, on the other hand, thought that the new *arrivals* had come to enslave them or to run them off their land. Thus, bitter and bloody clashes occurred which resulted in many deaths on both sides. The wars continued for several years until both sides realized that they were fighting a losing battle. They, therefore, decided to unite as a country and a people.

Following the end of the clashes, a new struggle started in Liberia—the class system. Embedded in the founders was the mentality of their old slave masters; they felt superior to the natives. Intermarriage was almost impossible. The founders felt that their brothers sold them into slavery because of what they were taught in America. They were not told the truth—that most of them were captured and taken to North America to work on the farms.

It is unfortunate that the class system gave room to discrimination, corruption, injustice and other malpractices, resulting in the April 12, 1980, coup in Liberia.

In the book, *Africa and Children,* the author has endeavored to demonstrate his vast knowledge of and keen interest in the development of children in Africa, particularly Liberia. Some Africans believe that every couple should have children, no matter what the cost; that children represent the new tomorrow.

The main character in the novel, Mary Tweh, does not only represent the new African woman, but she epitomizes the predominant two classes of people in Liberia—the settlers and the natives. Mary is married to Clinton Simpson not necessarily to have children, but because she is in love with her husband. She is not married to him because of his social standing in the community.

Ironically, Mary is discriminated against by some Monrovians because of her ethnic background. Mary is not considered as a "Monrovia girl."

Africa and Children is, therefore, an attempt to unearth some of the many ills in the Liberian society over the years: discrimination, corruption, nepotism, sectionalism, tribalism, civil liberties, press freedom, etc. The author has tried to provoke these and many more questions in a simple, understandable, readable and affordable manner. So, read on...

James T. Forte, Jr.

Preface

The idea to write this book was born at the close of the '70s when we were studying at the University of Liberia.

Most, if not all of the Literature texts we studied, were written by American, British, and a few African writers. The only Liberian novel we had at our disposal was Bai T. Moore's *Murder in the Cassava Patch*. For those of us who read English, the challenge was ours: to write and publish authentic Liberian literary works. That challenge still stands.

This attempt is designed to pay homage to both past and present Liberian authors and to encourage future Liberian writers. We invite your constructive criticisms, with the view of writing better novels in the future.

Chapter 1

The life history of Mary Tweh is unique and worthy of careful observation. Mary is a true representative of new Monrovia. Her gold earrings, lockets, chains, and bracelets alone are worth over seven thousand dollars. She wears seventy-five dollar shoes every day, and orders her clothes from Sears, Montgomery Ward, and other leading department stores in the United States and Europe. Her perfumes come from Paris, France on special order.

But Mary is not carried away by materialism. She knows that material things are temporary and meaningless, that they only have any value because we, by convention, attach importance to them. A diamond ring, for example, is worth nothing to my mother in her village in grand Gedeh County, Liberia, for she has never even seen or heard about diamonds; but a hardened criminal in New York or London would gladly kill me if he saw me with a diamond ring. He knows the value of a diamond through his association with the so-called civilized people of the civilized world. What a civilized society you and I are a part of!

Mary is the only surviving child of her parents' ten children. All her brothers and sisters died when they were very young. Most of them never reached age four. Her mother,

Mrs. Lucretia D. M. Tweh, represents old Monrovia, with a hundred and five years to her credit. Lucretia lived and witnessed about four different presidential administrations; and that means a lot in the life of one person, especially a woman who spent her whole life in one city.

Monrovia is the capital city of Liberia, West Africa. Even though Lucretia was born of a well-to-do family in Monrovia, she did not complete her high school education. She was a dropout of old Liberia College, now the University of Liberia. But old lady Lu, as she is affectionately known by most Monrovians, often associated herself with the graduates of old Liberia College.

Lu was two hours old when her mother died in childbirth. The father, the Rt. Hon. Dr. Deleato Mantarda, got married to another Monrovia woman who was ten years older than he. He had to get married in less than a year because, as an honorable man, it was mandatory that Mantarda had a wife in his home nearly all of the time.

Hon. Mantarda was very outspoken in governmental, church and social matters. He ran into political difficulties with the government and he was thrown into prison for over fifteen years, on the charge of treason. All his houses and rubber farm went to the government.

No one associated with Mantarda while he was in jail. Even his best friends did not visit him. Only his wife and children visited him once a week. No one or group of people could openly discuss the imprisonment of Mantarda. His family barely ate one meal in a day while Hon. Mantarda was in jail. The wife and children were as isolated as Mantarda was in prison.

When Mantarda was released from prison, he did not even know the road to his house. The streets in Monrovia were not paved when he went in jail, and most of them were paved when he got out. Mantarda cried, "Real blood," when

14

the jailer told him: "Hon. Mantarda, you are free as of to-day's date; there is no magnitude in your case; and therefore the head of state has pardoned you. You can go home."

"If I were not a strong man, I would have died in jail. Let us learn to be strong in our lives," Mantarda told his wife and children when he got home.

His wife and children started crying with him. The neighbors came around to see him; the radio stations and newspapers headlined the freedom story of Hon. Mantarda. But old man Mantarda barely made it when he came from jail. He died after five years of his freedom.

The father of Mary Tweh was born of a Kru fisherman in Sasstown, Liberia. Mary's grandfather, Weah-Doe Tweh, plied the coast of West Africa, including Sierra Leone, Ivory Coast, Ghana, and Nigeria, working aboard a ship; and young Doe went with his father at sea most of the time.

The Krus of Liberia are seagoing people. Since the sea is often associated with adventure and bravery, young Doe Tweh was almost born with sea-travelling instinct. He was hostile, aggressive and noisy.

Young Tweh left Sasstown aboard a ship that was bound for Hamburg, West Germany. The captain of the ship did not know about little Tweh until the ship arrived in Germany. Tweh had no travelling documents.

The captain of the ship was in serious trouble with the German Immigration; and when it was proven that the captain was not aware of the illicit rider, the German Immigration deported Tweh to Liberia, via Monrovia.

Tweh washed dishes aboard the ship that brought him from Germany to Liberia in order to pay for his meals. He was hardworking and frisky. Most of the crew liked him. They gave him old shirts and trousers. Tweh had put on considerable weight when he arrived in Monrovia.

Tweh knew no one in Monrovia. His only bet was that Kru people were to be at the dock working. Sure enough, there were hundreds of Kru people singing and working at the Free Port of Monrovia. When Tweh landed on the Monrovia soil, he listened and passed the workers as if he was hearing a strange dialect; he was afraid to run into more trouble at the dock area.

He went across the street at the dock and boarded a money bus which headed for New Kru Town. The driver of the bus came to a complete stop when he drove to the main entrance of the New Kru Town Road and announced, "New Kru Town." The women with their market bags and students with their books under their arms climbed down the bus. Common sense whispered to Tweh to leave the bus at the New Kru Town junction.

He passed a few houses and came to the Mobil Gas Station where he met old man Wesseh sitting and smoking his pipe. He knew Wesseh was a Kru man, just by looking at him. Tweh. greeted Mr. Wesseh and began to tell his story in Kru. Many persons, mostly women who were cooking, came around to hear Tweh's story. They felt sorry for him. Some people volunteered to shelter him. But old man Wesseh, whom he met first at the gas station, told the crowd that he and his wife would take Tweh as their own son.

Some women cried as Tweh was narrating his experiences to and from Germany. The women wept because they felt that their children could have been in the same boat as Tweh. The Krus are very generous and open-minded people. They are not selfish. They are generally nice, but fussy sometimes, if they are pushed to the wall.

Little Tweh was outgoing. He mastered the sea very well. He brought whole canoes full of fish every day. He could also drive. Everybody in New Kru Town admired him for his smartness. Very soon, Tweh became a very popular boy in the community.

He was a good fighter. Tweh could confront four or five boys at the same time without being beaten. And this is what the Kru people like the most. They take pleasure in fighting on the beach. They use the sand on the beach as one of their weapons in fighting.

He appealed to his guardians to allow him attend school in Monrovia. Old man Wesseh bought the required books and uniform for Tweh. With the fish that Tweh sold, he was able to help meet his school expenses. He had enough money to transport himself to and from school by bus.

He could only go to the afternoon division of Daniel E. Howard School due to work in the morning. Afternoon school made no difference to Tweh. He often remarked: "The school is one thing and the student another. It is the student that sells the school to the public, and not the school. The school is but a building and its name shines and lives on forever through the achievements of graduates."

Daniel E. Howard School is coeducational; there he met a good number of fresh and frisky Monrovia boys and girls, including Lucretia Mantarda.

Lucretia made coconut candies and corn bread every afternoon for sale. The first place she advertised her candies and bread was in the classroom. But she had to obtain the permission of the class president before she sold her products. And the class president was Doe Tweh.

The principal of the school on several occasions reprimanded Tweh for some disturbances in class due to student market negotiations. It was not easy on the part of Tweh, as a class president, to stop the students from buying and selling candies and corn bread in class. Yet the principal was very strict about discipline and he wanted perfect decorum in all the classes and on the school campus as a whole.

One day, Tweh categorically refused to allow any student to sell candies and bread in class. Tweh had to stop them to set leadership example. However, Lucretia's stepmother could not understand why Lu did not sell all of her candies and bread by the close of the school day. Lu did not enjoy her after-school meal; instead, she had to answer dozens of questions regarding the leftover candies and bread. Lu explained to her stepmother that the principal was very particular about the complaints of students, as a result of the campus market. But the stepmother was uncompromising.

Some stepmothers make life very gloomy and impossible for their stepchildren. Often there is a distinction between children in the same home. The ill-treated children would grow up with some kind of resentment against stepmothers, always feeling inferior to the beloved children.

However, in most cases, the beloved children turn out to become nothing in life. Most of them are a total disgrace to their parents, whose only family names the children bear.

The next school day came; each child in Lu's home, except the children of Lu's stepmother, had specific assignments to finish before going to school. She was a bit late to finish her work because of the heavy Monrovia rain.

The last bell for school went off at 12:25 p.m., and the principal allowed five-minute grace. Bad luck hooked the ship of Lu that afternoon. While running to be on time, Lu fell and broke the big candy jar.

It was not the responsibility of the principal or any one; it was just something that any normal person could have understood. Lu knew what was going to be her pay at home; she thought that her stepmother would not understand the situation. She began to sob bitterly, knowing what would happen to her at home after school.

Chapter 2

Lu was still crying when she arrived on campus. When she saw the principal standing by the gate, she wiped her eyes. But Principal Johnson knew that Lu had been crying.

He asked, "What is wrong with you, Lu?"

"I broke the candy jar while running to school, because I am late for school. I know that my Ma will beat me after school," she replied.

"Who is your mother?"

"Mrs. Mantarda."

"Oh, I see why you are weeping. Maybe she will not punish you after school. Definitely, you did not mean to break the jar; that was an accident."

"She would not understand, Mr. Johnson. She will surely beat me after school is over, no matter what I explain to her."

"Where is your father? Is he in the country? I could possibly contact your father instead."

"He is in town. But he can't say or do anything if that woman is ready to beat me and say all kinds of things about me and my dead mother."

"Okay, let us not go into that. It is too private. I know just what to do. I will drop her a note and send it to her by you after school. Would that help?"

"That could help, Mr. Johnson. But she will not accept the note from me, because she will have to ask me about the contents of the note; and I must explain it to her. Could you give it to one of the students?"

"Yes, I will give it to the president of our class."

"Thank you, Principal Johnson."

Even though Lu was ten minutes behind schedule, the principal allowed her to pass through the gate.

Lu was still afraid in class. She was very quiet, sitting all by herself in the corner.

The principal accordingly wrote the note and carried it into Lu's classroom.

When he opened the classroom door and saw that there was no teacher in class, Principal Johnson asked, "Who is the president of this class?"

"I am," replied Tweh.

"Please give this note to Mrs. Mantarda after school, for me; it is very important."

"Yes, Sir. I will deliver the note after school."

"But. . . but. . . but Mr. Johnson, Mrs. Mantarda's daughter is right in class here, in the corner. Why not give her the note?" inquired one of the frisky students.

"That is not your business. If I wanted to give the note to Lu, I would have done so." Mr. Johnson silenced the student.

Tweh walked with Lu after school to carry the note to Mrs. Mantarda. Mrs. Mantarda was sitting down, watching her time to see when Lu was coming from school. She stretched her neck longer when she saw that Lu was walking with a boy.

"Where are you going, little boy?" she asked.

"I am bringing a note for you," Tweh replied.

"From whom?"

"From the principal of Daniel E. Howard."

"What for?"

"I do not know, Ma."

"Okay, come up and bring me the letter, quick."

Tweh ran upstairs and gave the letter to the old lady. She got mad with Lu after she read the first three sentences of the note; she threw the note away.

"You mean... you mean Lucretia. . . come up here very fast," she shouted.

"Yes, Ma, let me drop my books in our room," Lu replied.

Instead of waiting until Lu arrived upstairs, Mrs. Mantarda started to complain in a very loud voice.

"You want to tell me a big woman like Lucretia can't hold anything in her hands? You mean she will break everything in this house? Please look for the candy jar as well as the money for the candies. I don't want plenty talking this evening. It seems that you do not like the idea of selling for me in school, because you think that you are woman now; and if I tell your father, he would not say a word."

When Mrs. Mantarda ran out of breath, Lu began, "No, Ma, I did not mean to break the jar. I fell down while running to school this afternoon because I was late."

"And what the hell made you late for school? I don't want to hear anything from you. This is not your first time breaking my jar. Last week you broke my plate, the plate my Ma gave me; and today again you broke my candy jar. I am not here to be buying things just for you to break," Mrs. Mantarda said.

Tweh was quite astonished about the reaction of Mrs. Mantarda. Since Tweh knew all about the difficulties students were encountering in selling candies and bread, he could not withhold his peace but to put in a word for Lu. He just could not stand the woman.

He said, "No, Ma, I think Lu is very serious about selling candies and bread in school, because I know what goes on in school between the principal and the students. I happen

21

to know all this because I am the president of our class; and the principal of our school is always punishing students for noise in class, as a result of selling in class. But I do not know the whole story concerning the jar. Maybe that took place out of class."

"Young man, I know what I am saying. Thank you for bringing me the note. She will surely receive severe punishment for breaking the candy jar."

"I beg you, Ma. I will never do it again," Lu cried.

Tweh was standing still, with his mouth opened wide in amazement. Mrs. Mantarda thought that Tweh was meddling in her domestic affairs.

"Get going, young man. I am being finished with you long time. What are you doing standing? Are you the judge advocate in this case?" Mrs. Mantarda raged.

"I am sorry, Mrs. Mantarda. I do not mean any harm," Tweh replied while backing out.

Tweh left with a bleeding heart. He could picture the hell which Lu was catching at home. He knew also that Lu was more than an ordinary bread seller in school, because she employed more business tactics and techniques than any of the children in school. On the average, Lu sold about three dollars worth of candies and seven dollars of bread each school day. Seemingly, Mrs. Mantarda did not appreciate Lucretia's financial contribution.

Tweh made representation of the issue to Principal Johnson the next school day, not really reporting Mrs. Mantarda to the principal. That was her private matter. And there was nothing either the principal or Tweh could do about it. Not even the father of Lu could do anything about what was going on at home. At home, Mr. Mantarda was one inch higher than a domestic servant.

All Principal Johnson could do was to appeal to the conscience of the termagant Mrs. Mantarda, but to no avail. Lu thereafter continued to sell her candies and bread, with no hard feelings toward her stepmother. She redoubled her efforts to sell more candies and bread than in previous months and years.

Tweh at the time had fallen in "sympathetic love" with Lucretia, because of her determination to work hard. Tweh used his little class-president influence to help Lu sell her wares faster, with a net sale of fifteen to seventeen dollars a day.

Mrs. Mantarda observed the increase in the sale of candies and bread, but she made no compliments in favor of Lu.

Lu in reciprocal manner recognized that Tweh was in love with her. But according to one of the norms of African women, she did not show any sign that she, too, had fallen in love with Tweh. At first Lu shunned Tweh, to the extent that she abused him on several occasions. But Tweh was adamant. He was determined like hell. And this is how a man should chase a woman; don't be downhearted the first time she tells you no or when she insinuates that she is not at all interested because she has a boyfriend. The "no" of a woman often means "yes," especially in romantic affairs.

Lucretia turned positive in about three weeks. As a gesture of "yes," she made extra candies and bread for Tweh; she used her own money to buy the ingredients for Tweh's bread and candies. Without any formal word of appeal with the words "I love you," Lu and Tweh became "play-play," boyfriend and girlfriend.

Tweh and Lu graduated from the elementary division of Daniel E. Howard. Lu's parents made arrangements for Lu to attend Liberia College; Lu wanted Tweh to enroll at the same school so that their relationship would grow even stronger at college level.

The love that grows from elementary days to high school and finally college, is worthy of becoming marital love. This

23

duration of a love affair is not however, the only yardstick of genuine love, or love that is built upon tested and solid grounds. School-day tenderness may turn to the opposite after marriage.

Lucretia knew very well that Tweh did not have the money to attend Liberia College. Since she had the means, it was her commitment to assist Tweh to enter the college in Monrovia.

She sent a message to Tweh so that he would meet her at a school dance. Tweh was not at home when the go-between whom Lu sent transmitted the message in New Kru Town. He was somewhere on the beach playing soccer. When Tweh got home, his guardians told him that a girl from Broad Street had sent him a message. But the messenger distorted the content of the message. The guardians in consequence could not arrange the intended message. Instead of saying that Lu wanted to see Tweh at the school dance at Sac Tower on United Nations Drive, the mediator said that Lu wanted to see Tweh at her home on Broad Street.

Tweh told his guardians that the message was not correct. It was quite hard to see a girl at her home without any previous knowledge or approval of her parents. Tweh was not fool enough to march up on Broad Street and climb the front or back door steps of Hon. Montarda to see his girl-friend. He decided not to go there at all. It is better to be absent and happy than to be present and miserable.

Lu had a bad evening because Tweh was not around. She did not even want to dance. Perhaps Tweh did not hear of the go-back-to-school dance at Sac Tower or else he would have gone there.

Time was running out for school to reopen.

One of the alternatives was to send some money to Tweh, covering his tuition, books, and uniform. Lu raked about one hundred fifty dollars from the pocket of her father and sent it to Tweh by the same mediator. She also enclosed a note, explaining her disappointment and the purpose of the money.

Tweh did not know what to say when he received the fat envelope from the messenger. In fact, Tweh had not owned one hundred fifty dollars at the same time. He was like a chicken without a head.

He said to the runner, "Say thanks to Lu. I will see her this week, say at the afternoon movies."

"What is that, Tweh?" asked his father.

"Pa, I am so happy that I just do not know what to do. One girl who graduated with me at Daniel E. Howard sent me one hundred fifty dollars for my school fees, books and uniform, to attend Liberia College, on Camp Johnson Road."

"Who is the girl? I hope that she did not steal the money, because it is too much," old man Wesseh said.

"No, Pa. She did not steal the money. Her father has got money. She is the daughter of Hon. Mantarda, the man who is living in the pink house on Broad Street, near the Baptist Church."

"Oh, I know him, my son. They are money people, even though that is our money. They are enjoying our taxes."

"And who is the girl to you?" asked Mrs. Wesseh.

"She is my girlfriend, Ma."

"That is good, son. But you should be nice to her, also. It takes a nice girl to do such. I hope that one day I will see her, just to say thanks to her. She may become my daughter-in-law in the future," Mrs. Wesseh added.

"Yes, Ma. I will be nice to her. I will make it possible to bring her here so you and Pa will see her. She would like to see you people also," Tweh said.

All went well according to plan. Tweh and Lu enrolled in the high school division of the college. The fact that Tweh entered Liberia College was a breakthrough not only for his family, but for all the Kru people. Liberia College was intended to nurture the children of the elite in Liberia, for leadership in state, business, and church affairs.

The two lovers tried to conceal their affair in school but it was not an easy task. The professors at the college knew the parents and social standing of Lu as well as the background of Tweh. They tried to equate the backgrounds of Tweh and Lu but the professors could not come to any compromise. The professors felt that Tweh and Lu were not homogeneous socially; yet Tweh and Lu were steering the same love boat to happiness.

The professors failed to know however, that Tweh had an international passport; he was one of the most brilliant students who had ever enrolled at Liberia College. He lectured his colleagues in the absence of geometry, mathematics and philosophy professors. He was better known in the school as "Barbie," or "Kruman," but a damn clever Kru man.

The parents of Lu could not approve of Tweh being their would-be son-in-law. Tweh knew that, too. He wanted to inform the parents of Lu, due to respect, but Lu advised him not to do so. She said that her parents would never accept Tweh and therefore there was no point trying to meet them personally and formally.

Love has no boundaries. You cannot stop Mary Victoria Curtis from falling in love with Flomo Dormah Kollie, simply because Kollie's parents are poor and illiterate. People would like to maintain their status quo - as it was yesterday, so shall it be today, tomorrow, and in the days and years ahead, no matter under what circumstances. But just as there are conservatives, so there exist liberals and radicals who from time to time challenge the beliefs and practices of the conservatives, and vice versa.

At any rate, Lucretia and Tweh helped themselves to the fruit of life, following an evening at a college dance. Lu had to socialize as a college student—that her parents could not stop her from doing. She would not have fallen into the hungry trap of Tweh that night if the senior class of Liberia College did not stage a dance to raise funds for a worthy cause.

That event opened the way for Lucretia's ten children, with no stopping or turning back. It seemed that Lu was in a marathon with her equals; she gave birth to a child every year, for ten consecutive years. Prestigious as it was, Lucretia would sit and tell people, "I have had ten children but only one is living; and yet I am going strong."

Chapter 3

No belly grows from the back. The belly of a pregnant woman and any one must protrude in the front, and not in the rear; but Lucretia Mantarda wanted to redirect the course of her belly, to hide it from her parents, schoolmates and the people in the neighborhood, but to no avail. The law of nature must take its course.

Lu did not see her period for three months after she and Tweh had their first sex session on the night of the school dance. Her breasts were as full as big German plums; the nipples of her breasts turned black, real black and pregnant with baby juice; milk gushed out of her breasts when she pressed them while she was all by herself in the bathroom. She was very moody most of the time during the first three months of her pregnancy. Lucretia was also irregular in attendance at school and the professors noticed her unexcused absence.

The seed that falls on fertile ground must germinate. Lu was a virgin, untouched at the time Tweh netted in her the first sperm on that memorable night, thus making her a full-fledged woman. Lucretia was on her way to becoming a mother, mother of a new baby boy or girl.

Her pregnancy was a scandal to the Mantarda family, especially to the ego of her father, a well-known churchman and politician in the country.

As a mature woman, the stepmother noticed that Lu was hiding something from her and the rest of the older girls at home. Lu would not go in the bathroom with the rest of the older girls; instead, she would visit the bathroom alone. Usually the bigger girls took baths together, especially when school was in session. Mrs. Mantarda noticed that Lu's mouth was juicy with saliva, one of the symptoms of pregnancy. But she would not spit, even if her mouth was filled with spit. She appeared to be under severe tension whenever the stepmother came around to supervise some domestic work in the kitchen.

The mother called Lu upstairs for secret questioning and a face-to-face talk.

"Lu, please come upstairs after your Pa is gone to work."

"Yes, Ma. I think that Pa is about ready to go to work. The driver has warmed the engine of the car. I think that Pa will soon finish eating his breakfast," Lu responded.

Lu suspected that her mother knew about the pregnancy. She thought to do one thing: to tell her mother the truth, that she was de-virginized by Doe Tweh. Lu was in a confused state of mind, as to whether one sex session would make a baby; she only knew theoretical biology, not the applied one.

When the driver zoomed the black Plymouth out of the yard, carrying Hon. Mantarda to work, Lu felt relieved. She had been afraid that her father had overheard what her mother had said in the kitchen. The father could hear so well that he could monitor two or three conversations at the same time. Luckily, he enjoyed his ham and bacon breakfast that morning so much that he could not hear anything that was being said three yards away from him.

There was no need, however, of being afraid that her father would hear of the pregnancy. What has come to the hearing of a wife, in some cases, I mean most cases, must come to the knowledge of the husband. Genuine wife and husband should be inseparable in some matters. In the Lucretia case, there was no way of hiding the embarrassing news from the father.

Mrs. Mantarda came downstairs to the kitchen, to see what the children, some of whom were washing, cooking, and cleaning, were doing. It was out of protocol that she had to come to see what the children were doing in the kitchen. Lu was in charge of all the affairs in the kitchen. She really came down to pass on a direct message to Lu.

She called Lu aside and whispered in her ear, "Bring two bottles of Coke from the refrigerator and follow me upstairs."

"Yes, Ma. I'll be there in a minute."

Lu and her Ma almost walked side by side upstairs; she hurriedly got the two Cokes, an opener and two saucers.

"Sit down on the bed, Lu, and open the Cokes, one for you and one for me."

"Yes, Ma."

While sipping her Coke, Mrs. Mantarda started the conversation.

"I bought for you some pieces, for your dresses. In fact, some of my Sunday dresses are two small for me; you can have them. I packed them already on the bed."

"Thanks very much, Ma," Lu said.

Lu could hardly swallow her Coke. Her stepmother was being too polite and kind that morning. And such generosity sparked greater fear in Lu. The Coke Lu was drinking tasted like silver in her mouth.

"Let's talk like equals," Mrs. Mantarda diverted the course of their conversation. "You are a college girl or woman now; and there should not be any difference between you and me; except that I am married, and you are still single. But you could get married today and go to school tomorrow. So, we are equals to some level. What I am about to ask you is highly confidential. Keep it to yourself. Don't tell any of the girls downstairs or your friends in school."

"What is it, Ma?" Lu inquired.

"Well. . . I am sure that you know what it means for a woman to see her period, right?"

"Yes, I know."

"You know also what it means when a woman does not see her period?"

"Not quite."

"You don't know, Lu?"

"No, I don't know."

"Did you menstruate last month?"

"Hum. . . hum. . . no, Ma."

"What do you think is the cause, Lu? Are you sick or something?"

"I do not know, Ma. But I am not sick, I mean sick to be in bed."

"But do you feel sick?"

"Kind of. But I would not call it sickness. I just feel funny and weak, especially in the stomach."

"Let me ask you another question. Have you gone to bed with a man? To that, do you have a boyfriend, who did a bad thing to you?"

"What do you call a bad thing?"

"I mean sex."

"Oh, I did not know that sex was a bad thing. Answering your first question, I have not gone to bed with any man. I have not even slept in a bed with any man in my life, except my father, when I was small. The second question, yes. I have a boyfriend in school. We are classmates."

"What is his name?"

"Doe Tweh."

"Doe Tweh? Where does he live? And where does he come from?"

"He is living in New Kru Town; he is Kru."

"Kru? What are you doing with a Kru man, Lu? Anyway, that is not the main issue for now. Listen, Lu, if I say gone to bed, I do not mean sleeping in bed with a man. I mean sex relations with your boyfriend or any man."

"What do you mean by sex relations, Ma?"

"You college woman, you want to tell me you do not know what sex relations means? He had sex with you?"

"Yes, Ma. But I did not sleep with him."

"That was enough sleeping with him. Look, Lu, tell me the truth. When was it that he had sex with you?"

"I can't remember the exact date. But it is about three months ago, say before school reopened in March this year. I can say at the close of February this year."

"My God! This is June. Three months gone. Since that time have you seen your period?"

"Why you did not tell me? Or what have you done about it?"

"Nothing. I have done nothing about it because I do not know what is wrong, much less to talk about what to do."

"Don't be disturbed about what I will tell you. This has happened to girls over the years, including girls in my school days, even the days of my mother, due to ignorance. I think that you are three months pregnant, Lu. You do not have to sleep with a man before you get pregnant, having had sex with him. You can have sex once and get trapped. I have noticed in recent weeks that you are not what you used to

32

be, not normal. And as a woman, experienced woman, too, I knew that you were pregnant. But I did not want to be fast."

Lu started shaking and crying. The idea that she was really pregnant frightened her. She could not believe it. Lu was confused- confused to the point that she spilled the coke which she was drinking.

"Stop crying, Lu. I am particularly disturbed, too, because of the shame and scandal which this pregnancy has brought to our family, the Mantarda family, in Monrovia. I know how these Monrovia people can gossip; they talk things that do not concern them.

"I do know how your father will react to this kind of shameful situation. But do not be afraid. I will tell your father as soon as possible, for I do not want your father to feel that I have been au courant with the whole issue from the beginning till now. I know him very well. I know that he will mishandle the boy. Definitely, we will have to call the boy and his people, if he has his people in Monrovia. He must marry you before the belly is big enough for the people in Monrovia to notice it.

"You see, Lu, we do not want any bastard in this family. We will never entertain any bastard in this family of ours. We have not done it and will not entertain such! Yet, we cannot even abort the belly. The human being in your stomach may become the next president of Liberia; who knows? Who knows whether that will be your last child, perhaps even a boy? And here we are crying for a boy in the family! Your father has only girls. But the so-called Tweh will have to marry you, by this week or next week. Go downstairs and be cool. I will inform your father about it, and he will not beat you either."

"Yes, Ma. I will try to be calm."

Lu went downstairs as if all were well. She went about her normal duties the whole day. But she did not go to school that day. Her mind was not composed enough to absorb any lessons that day in school.

One thing she did not forget to do was to rush a note to Doe Tweh in school. She explained to Tweh the whole situation, how she had not seen her period from the night of the go-back-to-school dance. She encouraged him, however, not to be afraid because she was ready to back him all the way through. She told him also that her stepmother, Mrs. Mantarda, had met with her and indicated that she and Tweh would get married, if it were proven that she was pregnant.

Doe Tweh did not hide the news from his parents in New Kru Town after he came from school that day. Old man Wesseh and his wife were not pleased about the embarrassing situation. But there was nothing they could do about it. They were afraid that Hon. Mantarda would ask Tweh to leave Monrovia or marry his daughter immediately, or he could also put Tweh in jail.

Tweh told his parents that he would meet with Hon. Mantarda and his wife as a man. "I will face the situation as a man; it is not criminal to impregnate any woman; it is only embarrassing to do so out of wedlock, for which I am very sorry. I will stand by the girl if it is true that she is pregnant by me."

Mrs. Mantarda stayed in bed the whole day. She was sick socially and morally, thinking how the people in Monrovia would look at the Mantarda family. She did not know how to break the news to the husband. The bad news could have sent old man Mantarda to his grave. He was suffering from hypertension and old age was against him already.

Mrs. Mantarda's heart beat faster when her husband drove in the yard from work. She had to exercise all her female ingenuity. Under the guise of being polite and romantic, she rushed to the door to kiss him welcome from work. She took off his coat and hat and asked him about the nature of his job that day. He could not say anything much so she thought that he was hungry and tired.

Chapter 4

"Children, get some cold water from the refrigerator for your Pa. I know that he is very hungry," she commanded the children.

One of the girls got the bottle of icy cold water from the refrigerator and placed it on the table. The food was already there, covered with a white table towel; everything was still warm.

It was when Mantarda smelled the food that he told his wife that the job was okay. He drew his big brown chair to destroy his meal for the day. Mrs. Mantarda sat beside him to keep him company while he was eating. She manufactured all kinds of conversation while her husband's jaws were filled with food like a gigantic jaw crusher, crushing iron ore into smaller pieces. Naturally, he could not fully participate in the conversation.

"You have not told me how nice the food is, honey," she said, rubbing his gray hair.

"Honey, the food is nice. Who cooked today?"

"Mary."

"Is Mary big enough to cook? Why didn't Lucretia cook?"

"Yes, Mary is big enough to cook; she has been cooking for the last four months. You have eaten her food several times. You can see how the food is nice today? Lu is not quite well today."

"What is wrong with her?"

"She is sick, suffering from a severe headache."

"She did not go to school today?"

"No."

"She saw the doctor?"

"No. I gave her some aspirin and I think that she is okay now."

"Honey, how was the job today?"

"Oh, the job is fine and hectic; I have not had any trouble with the old people, but they bring all their troubles to me, as they did today. It is really hard to work with people, especially the older ones, even though I am old myself."

"That is true. I think that you are tired and need complete rest, say a vacation. Why don't we go out this evening for a drink?"

"I am too tired to drive, honey. Maybe the driver will take us."

"No, let the driver go home. He has been working the whole day also and perhaps he is hungry and tired as well."

"If you say so, tell the driver to go home and you drive this evening."

Mrs. Mantarda instructed the driver to go home for the day, in fact for the week. That was on Friday.

Her husband ate his meal and had enough rest before they went out for a change.

The rendezvous was jammed to capacity; eminent citizens and their wives or girlfriends were there. Some of the people sitting in the darkest portion of the bar recognized Hon. Mantarda and his wife as soon as they entered. As a token of social recognition and respect, a few of his friends and lower level acquaintances offered them drinks, but Hon. Mantarda insisted that they buy their own drinks first. He and his wife joined some of their friends at a large rectangular table in the corner of the bar.

"Give me double shots of Mateus wine and a cold bottle of Club beer," he placed in his order.

The bartender hurriedly complied with his order. The Honorable advanced a toast of friendship and then, what seemed like a drinking competition started at the table. The atmosphere of the bar was conducive. In the bar such appealing music was being played that even the older people were placed in a dancing mood.

Mr. Mantarda killed four big bottles of Club beer in less than two hours, dancing and cracking old jokes. His table became the center of attraction. The table was crowded with both old and young people as he told familiar jokes, some depicting sex.

His wife tried to program his drinking that night, but he did not pay any heed to her. He was carried away by the music and the new dance that was in town. "Sweet Mother" was the popular record that night at the bar, in fact in the rest of Monrovia and Liberia as well.

He did not want to leave the bar early that night. Mrs. Mantarda insisted that they leave, even though it was a Friday night. He called for another beer, this time from the freezer, but he could not finish that beer. He was indeed fully saturated with alcohol for the night. The body cannot take any more than it can contain.

"Let's go home now, honey. That is enough for tonight," his wife told him.

"Where are we going?"

"We are going home. It is quite late to be here. Say, it is after two o'clock in the morning."

"But I am still enjoying myself. You can go home if you are tired. I can ask one of these boys to drop you home."

"No, I will not leave you here. We will go together."

"Okay, let's go. But I will drive. When we came, you drove. Now it is my time to drive you back home," he said.

"It is all right. I will drive back home. I think that you are a bit tired and sleepy."

"Okay, drive the car, but be careful. Even though you say that I am drunk, I am not a fool."

Mr. Mantarda was conversing discursively from the time they left the bar until they reached home. His wife simply agreed with him. The time was not ripe to unfurl the sour news about his daughter. She waited until the next morning before she tapped him on the shoulder.

"Wake up, honey. I have something important to tell you," she said.

"Hum.. . hum. . . what is it?" he asked, rolling from one side of the bed to the other.

"I want you to open your eyes. This is very important to you, the family and me. So get up and let us sit and talk this over."

"Okay, let me get up. What is it all about?"

"Well, I want to. . . what I am about to say is very shameful; and I do not want you to make noise about it. As a family we have got an image to keep in Monrovia and in the country. It is shameful because it should not have happened as it did. If you make noise about it, it will spread more than what it is now."

"Look, talk on; I am still sleepy. You know how late we stayed up last night. What has happened?"

"Our oldest daughter, Lucretia, is pregnant. She is three months gone. I just discovered this yesterday. That is the situation."

"What! For whom is she pregnant?"

"For one Doe Tweh, a Kru boy at the college."

"Kru boy?"

"Yes. He is Kru. This is what Lu told me yesterday morning."

"Well, he will have to marry her because there will be no bastard in this house, at least not when I am living! In fact, Lu will not live in this house! She should go to her man, 'cause she is a full woman now. Two women cannot be under the same roof. I mean by this week or next week they should get married. I will inform the Mr. Tweh and his people today so that they will come for their wife," Hon. Mantarda raised his voice.

"Don't talk so loud. Take it easy. You are not a well man, suffering from high blood pressure. It is not good for you to be annoyed. I think that what we should do is to call Dr. Semola this morning to examine Lu and find out for sure whether she is pregnant. We can then call the boy and tell him of the doctor's report."

"I think you are correct. We should contact our family doctor this morning."

The husband and wife did not sleep anymore that morning. He was mad indeed, to the point that he ran behind Lucretia with his pistol that morning to kill her. But his wife was very smart and managed to stop him from getting into trouble in the eyes of the law.

Lu ran from the house to her aunt on Snapper Hill. She explained everything to the aunt. The aunt was quite surprised that Lu was pregnant. Lu always looked so innocent, but she was far from being innocent sexually. It is only that a guilty man always wears an innocent face.

The aunt made matters worse for Lu. She alarmed all her relatives to come over and hear the story. The brothers, sisters, aunts, first and second cousins, all came over to hear the news.

"Lucretia is pregnant!"

"What?"

"Lucretia is pregnant, my people," the aunt proclaimed.

The family people rushed to the Broad Street home of Hon. Mantarda to find out the truth.

Of course, there was no way to lie about such a scandal. Some family members insisted that they call the government gynecologist, even though the father told them that the family doctor had earlier declared Lucretia pregnant. The doctor came and did not have to even employ his testing equipment. He told the family that Lu was three and a half months pregnant. The doctor was not wrong. This was in keeping with the timing of the go-back-to-school dance.

The old school from whence came old man Mantarda and his wife was, to some level, responsible for the pregnancy of Lucretia. The old folks would not tell their children the truth about sex and its consequences. They told their children that sex is absolutely bad and that children or young people who are not married should not engage in sexual activities.

Instead, the old people should have told their children that for the sake of social welfare, juvenile delinquency and morality, young girls who are not married should not get pregnant out of wedlock and that if a girl reaches puberty and has sex, she will surely get pregnant. Mothers in particular should play a leading role in educating their daughters. They should not hide the fact that sex is good. It is one of the enjoyable and exciting experiences of life. It is wrong to lie to children; children possess investigative minds and will learn the truth. And parents can explain to their children why illegitimate children can be a problem and a burden to the community.

This is why Liberian schools and schools in all developing countries should teach sex education in elementary and high schools, not to mention colleges and universities. Sex education is as essential today as any discipline taught in school.

The family of Lucretia had no right to blame the event on her. By consensus, the family agreed that Lu would get married to whosoever had impregnated her.

Mantarda was so disturbed that he wanted to face Tweh himself and tell him about the damage he had done to his daughter and to the image of his family. However, everyone knew that it would not be wise for him to go to New Kru Town himself; instead, one of the uncles and the driver went to New Kru Town to inform Tweh and his family.

The news did not hit the Tweh family too hard. Tweh had briefed his family on the matter. He told his parents that Lu was his girlfriend. He also mentioned to them that he would marry her any time. He knew her character.

The stepfather of Tweh rounded up some leading personalities in New Kru Town so that they would join with his wife and him to beg and hear the Mantarda family's side of the story. Among the wise men whom Wesseh contacted to sit in on the pregnancy matter was the Kru Governor, Nagbe Weakar Woljroh.

Governor Woljroh was a well-known figure, not only in Monrovia but throughout the country. His presence alone meant a lot to settling the palaver easily, not a real palaver in the true sense of the word. It was a family matter.

Family people may fight fist-to-fist today and become one body tomorrow.

The Broad Street home of Hon. Mantarda was the scene of the family investigation. Top men of the Mantarda family were present in full. They wanted to hear from Tweh and, most importantly, to judge him socially and intellectually. Hon. Mantarda and his family did not want to give away their daughter in marriage without knowing the background of the man.

Hon. Mantarda was reluctant to institute any stern action against Doe Tweh when he saw Governor Woljroh walked in with Tweh and the Wesseh family.

"What is the Kru Governor doing here tonight?" Hon. Mantarda asked jokingly.

"We are your visitors, Honorable," Woljroh replied, laughing.

"Have seats, ladies and gentlemen. This is what I can see. I think this is your second time in here, even though we should be good friends, years far back. The last time I believe you were here was during one inauguration of the late President Tubman. I think that was during his second inauguration but we are still friends," Hon. Mantarda added.

"That is true. But I cannot remember seeing you in my place in New Kru Town, if we have to be specific about visitation. Isn't it true?"

"You are correct, Governor. I cannot give you any good excuse for not coming to visit you one day in New Kru Town. You will see me very soon at your place."

Woljroh added, "You should know that we are here for an important matter, the end of which, I hope, will unite us as one family."

All this time, old man Wesseh and his wife could not say a word. They were afraid; Tweh also sat there, simply listening to the dialogue between the host and Governor Woljroh.

Chapter 5

Mantarda opened the talk. Addressing the Governor and the Wesseh family he said, "We are not here for long. The matter should be very short and sweet. The gentleman, Mr. Tweh, is supposed to be the boyfriend of our oldest daughter, Lucretia, who is sitting in the corner over there. She told us just yesterday that she is pregnant for Doe Tweh, the son of old man Wesseh.

"Now, as parents, my wife and I, including all my immediate family members, are concerned; this is a school girl. She was about to enter the college division of Liberia College. Now she is spoiled. She cannot go to school any more. Definitely, the doer of this action will have to marry her. The doer happens to be Tweh, according to Lucretia. Of course, I do not know whether she is telling the truth or not. Governor Woljroh and old man Wesseh, kindly ask your son whether he knows anything about this pregnancy."

"Thank you, Hon. Mantarda," Woljroh responded. "Wesseh, the father, explained the whole matter to me just this evening, and this is why we are here tonight. We do understand, as parents with children, how you and your wife feel about the condition of your daughter. We beg that you control yourselves as we ask Tweh.. Tweh, do you know this girl, Lucretia?"

"Yes, I know her," Tweh replied.

"Where do you know her?"

"In school. We have been classmates from Daniel E. Howard to Liberia College."

"Besides being classmates, do you have any other relations with her?"

"Yes."

"What is it?"

"She is my girlfriend."

"That is good. You listened and heard what the father of Lucretia said a few minutes ago. He said that Lu is pregnant for you. What have you to say?"

"Well, Governor, I would not say yes or no to the question. While it is true that Lu is my girlfriend, I do not know whether she is pregnant at this time. Now listen. She may be pregnant, according to the father, but I do not know. I must admit, however, that I had something to do with her. I would not deny that. But that she is pregnant for me, I do not know. She may be telling the truth."

"I want to believe that Tweh is a gentleman," Hon. Mantarda interrupted. "That he did not deny the fact that my daughter is his girlfriend is a sufficient ground that he is a man of his word. Not many of these frisky little boys in Monrovia would have been brave enough to tell us the truth. He is correct to say that he does not know of the pregnancy; perhaps Lucretia has not told him. In any case, this is why we have called you, Tweh, and your family to inform you officially of the situation and what decision my family has come to."

"Let me explain further, Hon. Mantarda," Tweh continued "This is not a boast. I have known this girl for a very long time.

And I didn't want such a thing as this to tarnish our relationship now or in the future. May I ask a question?"

"Go right ahead, Tweh," Mrs. Mantarda said.

"How do you know that she is pregnant and for how long is she pregnant?"

"We know through investigation, by asking her what is wrong with her. She has been sick in recent months. We carried her to the doctor who pronounced her three and a half months pregnant. And Lu told us that she does not know any other man or boy but you."

"I think that Lu is correct," Tweh said. "Governor, I would like to say that it is better to tell the truth than to evade it. I want to say here that Lu did not lie on me; she has told nothing but the truth. To Hon. Mantarda, his wife and family, I would like to apologize for the embarrassment which I have caused them through this pregnancy. I am in the wrong and I ask their forgiveness. I did not mean to embarrass you. It was due to a mistake and ignorance on our part. Please forgive me. I am willing to marry the girl anytime, but the important thing for now is your forgiveness."

Governor Woljroh added, "Hon. Mantarda, you, your wife and family have heard what Tweh said. We join with him to beg you. He has agreed to marry Lucretia. We are very, very sorry for the embarrassing situation."

Hon. Mantarda said on behalf of his family, "I feel that Tweh has broken our backbone. There is nothing that the family, or I in particular, have to say at this junction. He has apologized to my wife, the family and me. He has agreed to marry the girl. He has admitted his wrong. What else can we say here? The Bible clearly says that 'A kind word turneth

47

away wrath;' and this is what Tweh has demonstrated here tonight. We will, as soon as possible, arrange for the wedding, and Tweh can continue to go to school at the college. Who knows what will be the result of the pregnancy? Maybe it will be a boy. Here I am without a boy in the whole family. Everything is finished. Tweh is our son."

Old man Wesseh and his wife could not believe that the matter would be that short. They expressed their thanks and joy to the Mantarda family through the Governor. The issue was resolved amicably. That was the beginning of a strong family tie.

The Tweh-Lucretia wedding was the talk of the town. It was the wedding of the year. Mantarda and his wife made the name of their *family* known socially, financially, and politically, through the wedding of their first daughter. The wedding was so elaborate that nearly all the big shots in Monrovia attended; the academicians from Liberia College and Cuttington College were in full attendance. The majority of the Krus in New, Clara and Logan Towns attended the family knot-tying ceremonies

The people in Monrovia knew that it was a "shot-gun" wedding. Lucretia was pregnant and her family wanted to avoid scandal. There were several reasons why the wedding was so grand. It was shocking to Monrovians for a school girl, especially a girl at Liberia College, to get married suddenly without any protracted period of courtship. Then, too, the combination was very odd - a Kru man marrying a girl from the very heart of Monrovia. The union was unusual and therefore most people went to the wedding to see the gentlemen who broke the record of the so-called civilized marriage.

Those who are born in Monrovia call themselves "Rock town boys and girls." To some level, they feel superior to the rest of the people who are not born in Monrovia. Also, some citizens who are born in the coastal cities and suburban Monrovia have the same mentality of superiority over the people born in rural areas.

This is gross illiteracy on their part. Monrovia is not Liberia. It is only the capital city of the country, a minute fraction of the country. Being born in Monrovia and its suburbs does not mean that one would automatically make a substantial contribution towards the social and economic as well as educational advancement of the country.

There is nothing wrong with being proud of one's birthplace but when this pride is at the expense, disadvantage, and detriment of others, then it is questioned by not only the victims, but by outsiders as well.

The father of Lucretia volunteered to shoulder all the financial burdens of the wedding, but Tweh refused the generous offer. Tweh had a good savings account with the Bank of Monrovia, now First National City Bank of New York. The bank willingly granted Tweh a $5,000 loan, payable in three years. He was a good and dependable customer of the bank.

Mantarda and his wife went further than offering cash to Tweh. They prepared the first floor of their home for Tweh and his wife. The first floor contained two apartments with four bedrooms, two bathrooms, and two kitchens

Again, Tweh turned down the first floor apartment. He felt that as a married man, it was his sole obligation to shelter and feed his wife and family; that in order to steer the course of his family, it was his responsibility to support his family, and no one else's.

African housewives are submissive to their husbands because the husbands are responsible for the livelihood of the families. The husbands do most of the hard manual labor on their farms; they provide the meat and fish by hunting and fishing. And the husbands defend their families in time of war.

The man who supports you solely is your "small god" on earth. You have got to respect and honor him; you have got to do what he says. This is why underdeveloped or developing countries are, to a larger degree, submissive to the powerful countries of the world.

In our modern economy, the majority of African husbands earn higher salaries than their wives. The reasons are numerous. Some African women were not allowed to go to school; thus illiteracy is high among African women. Some African women who are educated are not allowed to work in offices and factories; rather, they take care of domestic affairs.

Offices and work sites are proven to be among the breeding places for corruption. Some career women are from time to time victimized by their boss men. The secretary-boss man relationship breaks some families, especially when the secretaries are given assignments to work overtime until 9:00 to 10:00 p.m. Some Africans who tend to be jealous do not allow their wives to work, especially not in offices.

There is nothing wrong with housewives working. If women will work, which they are doing, they should know their limitations. They should not challenge the rulings and decisions of their husbands at home.

Our women today, however, compete with us. Some are ministers, even prime ministers, lawyers, engineers, and doctors. These professions have their negative results. They make our women artificial. Some of our housewives cannot cook, and a woman who does not know how to cook is of no use to her husband- I mean African husband.

The situation is different in the western world, especially in the United States, where the husbands and housewives cook by turns; sometimes they even eat Burger Kings for the whole day. Tweh knew the requirement of his own society. If Lucretia was to play a major economic role in providing for their housing through the father, Tweh would not have had a say in the administration of his family affairs. Lu's father and mother could have walked into their apartment and dictated to Tweh how he should manage his domestic affairs. A proud man would never succumb to becoming a secondary leader in his own home, his own castle.

Tweh made arrangements to rent one of the modern apartments on Ashman Street, for fifty dollars per month. He told Lucretia about the apartment before the wedding. But Lu suggested that they live in the two apartments made available by her father. Tweh insisted that he was not moving in with the Mantarda family.

Lu brought up the housing issue during the last family meeting before the wedding. She explained to her father that Tweh did not seem to buy the idea of living on the first floor, which the father had prepared for them.

Expressing his amazement for Tweh's refusing the apartment Mantarda said, "My son, we do not mean to support you and your wife. We do know that you are still in school, hence it would be difficult for you to rent a decent place for now. This is why my wife and I decided to renovate the whole downstairs for you and Lucretia until you are financially strong enough to be on your own feet. I think it is not a disgrace for you and your wife to be here with us for a while."

Tweh replied, "We do not bluntly refuse your offer, Sir; but we feel that it is, and it should be, our responsibility to shoulder most, if not all of our family burdens. It is something that we will have to live with, whether you are around or not. My Pa, old man Wesseh, also offered me two rooms in his house; I turned them down, too. It is not that I am proud, but I would like to be responsible for my family. If at any time we need assistance, we will not hesitate to call on you."

"Where then will you live?" asked Mrs. Mantarda.

"We will live on Ashmun Street, near the College of West Africa. I am renting one apartment from Solommatus Cooper, for fifty dollars per month."

"That is too expensive," the father said. "How are you going to pay your rent?"

"I am being employed by Liberia College, as part-time mathematics instructor, with a starting salary of two hundred twenty-five dollars."

"That is not quite sufficient for you and your wife. You know that she will soon have a baby, making it three persons in the family.... Besides teaching, what else can you do?" Mantarda asked.

"I can type very well."

"How many words can you type per minute?"

"Fifty to seventy-five words per minute." -

"Have you worked before as a typist?"

"Yes. I had a vacation job with the Department of Interior, as a clerk/typist."

"Is that so?"

"Yes. The Secretary requested that I work with him directly, full-time; but I could not because I am still in school."

"The Secretary is my personal friend. I can talk with him today so that you will work with him as of next week, on a part-time basis; you cannot leave your school just for that. Definitely, he will give you the job if he hears my voice on the telephone."

Hon. Mantarda contacted the Interior Secretary and the job was secured the same day.

The wedding took place on schedule; the reception was held at the Monrovia City Hall. The motorcade with some three hundred cars took the main routes in Monrovia, including Broad, Randall, Center, Carey and Macdonald Streets; Camp Johnson Road, United Nations Drive and Tubman Boulevard.

The radio and TV audience could not readily picture Tweh; the wedding was among the news headlines of the day, with the Lucretia angle of the story being grossly magnified. Some of the audience referred to Tweh as a "country Kru boy" who wanted social and political acceptance by marrying Lucretia Mantarda. The gossipers, as in most cases, did not know the whole story behind the wedding.

Tweh and Lucretia became husband and wife! What? Tweh is married to Lucretia? That was the news in Monrovia for the whole week and the whole month.

Chapter 6

Tweh was then a full man, ready to face the reality of life, to program and direct the course of his *family,* to raise children and to train the children in the right direction.

Lucretia gave birth to their first child five months after the wedding.

Tweh was about to go to school that morning when Lucretia's stomach signaled that it was time for the baby to bounce on earth. He suspended classes that day and took his wife to the Catholic Hospital in a taxi cab; he was so nervous that he forgot to inform his parents-in-law.

The attending doctor was very scrupulous in handling Lu's case. She was crying in the corridor and delivery room, for help. No one could help her.

Tweh was with the doctor and the nurses when Lu delivered the nine and half pounds baby boy. He was so happy to see his own image, a boy, the dream of a proud father.

He took a taxi from the hospital to downtown Monrovia to buy some cigars that a man was born in his family. He lit one cigar in the store and began to puff it. He lit one cigar for the Lebanese merchant from whom he bought it and said, "Have a cigar to smoke. My wife delivered about half an hour ago, a baby boy. This is the beginning of the celebration".

The father-in-law cried for joy when he saw Tweh with a cigar in his mouth. Mantarda knew the whole story when he saw the cigar.

"God has not slept, my son," Mantarda jumped from his big, brown, easy chair. "We have a grandchild. A son is born in the Mantarda family for the first time; God is good, my people."

The whole Mantarda family immediately went to the Catholic Hospital to see the mother and the baby. The baby was crying when they arrived at the hospital; Mantarda could not believe his eyes.

He took the one-hour old baby from the bed and spat on his forehead four different times. He said, "A man must remain a man all of the time. We have not seen half a man. Man has always been a whole man; man has got to be resourceful, dependable and aggressive, and I want you to be just these qualities. As my first grandchild and the only son in the family, I, Dealato Mantarda, on behalf of my family and the Tweh family, name you after myself. The second child of Lu and Tweh will also be a boy; and he will be named after the father, Tweh."

Mantarda's wife and children danced in the hospital yard. Passersby came to see what was happening. A boy has been born in the Mantarda family!

Hon. Mantarda and his wife gave Tweh a purse of four hundred dollars for the mother and baby. They also told Tweh that their third daughter, Willella, would live with them to take care of the baby.

Tweh had bought all the baby things: Johnson baby oil and powder, blankets, diapers, shoes, bed, pins, etc. He also bought for his wife a new Opel sedan, as a gift for the delivery. The Opel was their first car.

He could afford to buy a car for his wife; Tweh maintained two jobs. He had the teaching job at Liberia College and the clerk/ typist job at the Department of Interior. His disposable income at the end of every month was over five hundred eighty dollars.

When the news of the new baby got to New Kru Town, over four buses of Kru women came to the Ashmun Street apartment of Tweh and the Catholic Hospital in Sinkor to see the baby and the mother; the Kru women made reasonable noise, singing SeoLilly, a popular and familiar Kru song. The women brought gifts for both the mother and the baby.

Mr. and Mrs. Wesseh led the group of dancers to the Ashmun street apartment because some of the people did not know where Tweh and his wife were living; Lucretia did not allow some relatives of Tweh to visit them on Ashmun Street. She often referred to them as "country people" and she was not prepared to entertain country people in her home.

Tweh did not bother himself ; the country people were his people, no matter what education he got, where he lived, or to whom he was married.

The Tweh and Mantarda families prized the little boy highly; the first child in a family is often given careful attention and love. But a human being is like a flower which may die any time. The Tweh baby did not live long; he died in his seventh month.

What a tragedy for the Tweh and Mantarda families!

The grief for the untimely death of the baby almost sent old man Mantarda six feet under. He took sick for months and could not believe that the baby was really dead.

People often make such a mistake, thinking that their relatives, wives or husbands will never die. Death is inevitable. There is no special time for death to creep in. We should be ready to accept it at any time with fortitude.

Perhaps what causes the phobia is that no one has died and come back to tell the story of the other world. Even the Christians who should be comforted by the knowledge that they will join their Father, with Jesus sitting on his right hand, are afraid of death. Why? Why should people be afraid of death if they proclaim that the world after death is by far better than the present one?

Whether we are afraid of death or not, it has got to come, just as surely as we were born. I feel that we should cry if one is born, because it is then that one's troubles begin on earth.

The bereaved families had one consolation; Tweh and Lu were still young. Tweh worked toward his marital commitment too. Lu gave birth to a child every one and a half years. She could never rest for two years at a time. When Tweh was in college alone, they had four children: all boys. But all died under age four.

Birth control was a novelty. It was unthinkable to stop a woman from having a baby. It was believed that children come from God and no one should do anything to impede the work of God.

After he left college and was fully employed by the Interior Department as clerk/typist, they had additional two boys and three girls and all these died also.

Tweh won the confidence of the Secretary of Interior, having worked efficiently at the Department for over three years. He was promoted to Provincial Commissioner, in charge of the then Eastern, Central and Western Provinces, now Grand Gedeh, Bong, Nimba and Lofa Counties.

The position of Provincial Commissioner took Tweh to many places in the interior of Liberia. There he came in close contact with the indigenous people of the country, most of whom believe in juju; they always consulted the witch doctor in time of trouble or seeming difficulties.

By way of conversation Tweh narrated the story of his wife and his dead children to some of his friends in Zorzor, Lofa County. The friends told him that someone in the neighborhood was responsible for all this tragedy in his family.

Tweh did not believe what his friends told him; he said that he was a Christian and did not believe in juju.

Jallah Yanquoi elaborated, "Christianity has got its place in Europe, Asia, America and Africa, as well as the world at large. But there are some beliefs which Christianity should not affect in Africa. All of us sitting here are Christians in our hearts, if not more Christian than the so-called Christians (God's chosen people) from America and Europe. Rubbing raw leaves from the bush, consulting the witch doctor, or wearing a rope around the waist has got nothing to do with Christianity, as far as I am concerned.

"A man who wears a medicine rope around his waist to protect himself, who welcomes strangers in his home; who visits bereaved stricken families; who marries two to ten wives without having girlfriends outside will sooner see God than a man with one wife and twenty girlfriends; a man who would not invite you to his place unless you give him a ring; a man who would give you a newspaper to read while he and his family eat at the table. Such a man, in my opinion, is not a Christian.

"I happen to know all of these facts because we have here in Zorzor some white missionaries who would not even give you an empty can to drink out of on the farm. They are mean, mean to the extent that we wonder why they came here to preach and convert us to Christianity. While it is true that they have built schools and hospitals for our people, their day-to-day relations with the people here is nil. In fact, the money for the running of the schools and hospitals, I believe, come from America, from members of their church, some of whom have not visited Africa. The donors of the money are Christians; they want to help the poor and needy in Africa; but the people to whom the money is entrusted are not Christians."

"You may be correct, Yanquoi; but you are talking about those who preach the gospel and not the message of the gospel," Tweh rebutted.

"If those who preach the gospel cannot do what the Bible says, how can they convince us, the nonbelievers?" Zayzay asked. "I will call the Zoe in a minute and he will explain to you, Commissioner Tweh, what we are saying to you. We do not say that you may not be Christian; but we want you to be an African Christian. I know that some of your Christian brothers and sisters come from all over Liberia to visit the Zoe in Zorzor for promotion on the job, fertility, and fortune telling.

"I know that you got married in church, with an open declaration that you would keep only that one wife. But you have girlfriends right here in Zorzor, some in Sanniquellie, Gbarnga, Tchien, not to mention Monrovia where you are living. I do have four wives with me presently; and I am satisfied with them. They give me all I need, my twenty children; they cook for me every day; they do some of the work on my farm, etc. Is that right, Commissioner, to have so many women all over the country, but still claim an official one wife?"

"I do not know exactly what to say, Zayzay. But it is better to have one wife than to have more than one. It is impossible to please two or more wives," Tweh said.

"Is it possible to please one wife and some twenty girlfriends?" Yanquoi inquired.

59

"Of course not. But we do have the girlfriends, because we just cannot resist the temptation of the women. We have fine girls coming up all the time; and it is hard to ignore them.... Let's forget about the women and talk about the Zoe. Who is he and what are his responsibilities in Zorzor?" Tweh asked.

"Zoe is the Presiding Officer and Supreme Commander of the Juju Guild. He is versatile in country medicine; he cures people with diseases; he tells fortunes; he can tell you what will happen to you in the future," Yanquoi explained.

"I would like to see him personally in order to be convinced," Tweh replied.

Fumbah beckoned to the Zoe while he was passing by on his way into the bush for some medicines. He came over without any questions. Yanquoi explained to the Zoe the nature of the argument and the status of Tweh in Liberia.

Since Tweh was doubtful, the Zoe did not ask him to explain anything concerning his life history and experience. The Zoe simply sent for his working medicine box to prove to Tweh that the "green leaf' has got power. He told Tweh that the medicines in bottles come from green leaves; the only difference is the methods of application.

The Zoe instructed Tweh to stand on a leopard skin with a plate of cold water in his two hands. He looked in the clear cold water and began to tell Tweh all about his school life, children, wife and even to forecast his future.

Lucretia had nine children, six boys and three girls; and all died. The Zoe saw the children in the plate.

The Zoe asked Tweh, "Is it true that your wife had nine children, three girls and six boys and they all died?"

"Yes. It is true."

"Is it true that your first child was a boy and he died under one year?"

"Yes."

"The last child of your wife was a girl and she died under five months. True or false?"

"True."

"You attended the biggest school of the government in Monrovia and you graduated with high honors. True or false?"

"True."

"Do you want me to tell you what have been the cause for the short illness of your children, and the cause of their death?"

"I will be happy if you tell me."

"I will tell you all.... In your neighborhood is a tall, bright lady; she is very kind and friendly to everyone, even to the children in the neighborhood. She has four boys. One of her children is an eminent citizen in Monrovia and in the country. She is killing all your children, including those of people near your apartment. She turns into a dragon in the night and sucks the blood of babies and young children. The lady has killed over thirty children in the neighborhood. Is it not true that during the last two months, some seven children died in your neighborhood?"

"I want to believe what you have just said because in recent weeks many children died on Ashmun Street. My only problem is that my wife and father-in-law will not believe me if I tell them the story in Monrovia. This is my only fear."

"Don't worry about what your wife or father-in-law will say. Tell them that the Zoe in Zorzor would like to see all of them, including the wife of Mantarda. I will tell you more if you return. Maybe your father-in-law has heard about me. I know all the big shots in Monrovia. They all come here in Zorzor to see me. As simple as I am, I am known by all your big shots in Monrovia and throughout the country."

Commissioner Tweh hauled out a twenty dollar bill from his wallet to give it to the Zoe. The Zoe did not take the money. He requested for a piece of kola. Tweh had no kola with him and the Zoe directed him to get it from someone in the audience.

Commissioner Tweh contacted the Lutheran Mission to have the mission plane at his disposal. He flew to Monrovia earlier than his official trip would have lasted to deliver the message to his parents-in-law and wife.

Hon. Mantarda was so happy to hear that the Zoe in Zorzor was willing to help his daughter and son-in-law. He had no cause to doubt the Zoe because he had himself visited many medicine men in Gibi, Buchanan and Bomi Hills.

The village, Gibi, is almost synonymous with juju and country medicine in Liberia. Some big shots in Monrovia and other cities in Liberia often go to Gibi for juju. Mantarda was a stern believer in juju, besides being a strong politician and churchman

Mrs. Mantarda and Lucretia were also enthusiastic about finding a solution to the tragedy in the Tweh family. They expressed willingness to travel to Zorzor in order to see the Zoe. The father-in-law sponsored the round trip. He chartered a special plane to carry them to Zorzor the next day.

Chapter 7

But when they arrived in Zorzor, the Zoe categorically refused to see them that day. Instead, he prepared a special hut for the strangers. No beds were in the hut. He told them through his messenger that they should sleep on the bare floor; and that he would see them the next morning.

He called on them at 4:30 the next morning.

The Zoe told the fortune seekers, "I knew that all of you were coming without hesitation. But Tweh's wife has doubts about me. However, I will try my best, beginning first with the father and mother of Lucretia. . . the father of Lu has not had any boy in his life. His first wife had Lucretia for him; and his present wife has three girls for him. So Lucretia is his oldest daughter. If all these facts are not true, please stop and correct me."

"No, go right ahead. All you have said is true and there is no need to doubt you; you have told nothing but the truth," Mantarda said.

"I will go further," the Zoe continued. "As I told Tweh, there is a bright lady near Tweh's apartment who is killing the children of Lucretia. She is a dragon in the night and sucks the blood of babies or young children. But Lucretia will have a girl. I mean she will get pregnant in three months and the pregnancy will be a girl. The same lady will make an attempt to destroy the pregnancy; but she will surely die. The death of the witch will be very sudden. She will get sick and drop in the street; she will die in the morning."

"The pregnancy will be the last of Lu. After the delivery of the girl, Lucretia will never menstruate again in her life. In fact, Tweh will never have any boy, even if he has sexual relations with other women. The last girl child will be as strong as a man; we call such a woman 'man-woman.' The last child will grow to get married and will not have any child with her first husband. He will pre-decease her. It is unfortunate to note that Tweh will not live long enough to see the last child at age fifteen. Tweh will die by accident'

"No! That is not true! My husband will not die by accident!" Lucretia shouted.

"Gamblers bet for money and material things when playing games. But no gambler can bet that the future will not come; the future has got to come. The first sign is that the bright lady will be the first to greet Tweh and Lucretia when they return to Monrovia; if she will not be the first to say hello to you on your return to Monrovia, then I am the captain of all the liars in the world," the Zoe said.

Everybody grew tense. No one could say anything. "There is nothing I have to say at this junction; here is a calabash of medicine. All of you should drink from this calabash and finish all the medicine. If you do not finish the medicine, your mission here will be a fiasco. I do not need any pay from you. If you want to, you can send it to me later after you have proven that what I said is true," the Zoe concluded

Again, the Zoe locked the mouths of Montarda, his wife, Lucretia and Tweh.

No one dares to disprove the declarations of the Zoe. If you have doubts about the forecasts of the Zoe, it is better to conceal your doubts than to tell the villagers or the tribesmen that the Zoe is lying. Challenging the Zoe is like confronting the whole village or tribe.

The Zoe told the truth. Everything he said became a reality when they returned to Monrovia. The bright lady was the first to meet and greet Tweh and Lucretia on their return to Monrovia. But the power of the juju drove the lady away very fast.

Lucretia missed her period in the third month. Precisely at the close of the third month, Lu was pregnant. She told Tweh that she missed her period and Tweh suggested that they wait for two to three weeks before consulting the doctor. When the doctor examined Lucretia after the three weeks, Lu was declared pregnant.

Lucretia could not believe that she was pregnant. She and Tweh drove to the home of old man Mantarda and explained what the doctor said. The second forecast of the Zoe had come true. Lucretia got pregnant in three months.

Tweh took the mission plane again to go to Zorzor to express his confidence in the Zoe. The medicine man was also happy to see Tweh back in three months, following the first consultation.

"What is the news in Monrovia, my Son?" the Zoe asked Tweh. "There is good news in Monrovia. This is why I am here to see you. You told us that my wife would get pregnant in three months. We took her to the doctor yesterday and the doctor said she is pregnant."

"I told you that your wife would get pregnant in three months; except that you did not believe me. The only thing about us is that we do not blow our own trumpet. We have been a Zoe for over thirty-five years. Maybe you were not even born when I started this job. We specialize in the 'green leaf' just as you know your book. No one taught me country medicine. I had a dream one day and someone taught me all the medicine I know. And that is how I became a Zoe."

"Yes. You really understand the leaf. My wife and I as well as my parents-in-law do not know how to thank you. We are not paying you for the job you have done so far. We brought you a little purse of two hundred dollars for your 'cold water.' We are friends as of today's date because we will, from time to time, call on you for help."

"I told you earlier that I do not charge my clients. In fact, I don't usually take money from people. I usually receive goats, chickens or cows, not money. However, I shall not refuse what you brought me. But I will not take all the money. I will only take $75.00 of the money. You can take the rest back to your wife and family. The money is too much. *I* will not take all."

"No, my wife and *I* brought this little purse for you. Have all the money. We appropriated it for you."

"I have told you that *I* will take only seventy five dollars of the money. This is not my own decision. It is the decision of the Juju Guild of which I am only the chairman. I don't do things on my own. I have got to obey. Obedience is one of the cardinal principles of the Juju Guild, and I would not do anything to the contrary."

The Zoe has the last saying, especially in his chambers. He gave Tweh a black rope for Lucretia to tie on her waist. He said, "The bright lady will try by all means to suck the blood of the baby in the womb of your wife. But with the black rope, the lady must fail. With the rope on the waist of Lucretia, the lady will never enter your apartment until her death."

Tweh explained the usage of the black rope to Lucretia when he returned to Monrovia. Lu felt happy and secure wearing it.

Five months passed and the wicked lady did not visit Lucretia as she used to do in the past. She did not come by their apartment to see and welcome the newborn baby; and that was very unusual on her part. Everybody else in the neighborhood brought gifts to the baby and mother.

"Honey, I think that Luciano Hamilton is the lady that the Zoe referred to when we visited him in Zorzor," Lu said to Tweh.

"Of course, yes. Who else? She is the one and everybody around here knows now; I told them what the Zoe explained to us in Zorzor. The people in the neighborhood have seen it for themselves because Luciano has not come here for five months, especially since you delivered. The Zoe must be a powerful medicine man, indeed."

"If that be the case, why can't we go back to the Zoe and ask him to do something about your case? Remember, he told us that you will die in an accident; even though I disagreed with him when he told us. But I am convinced now that what he said might be true in the future."

"No, Lu. Everything is up to God. I have no fear about any accident. If any accident should occur, it must be commissioned by God and nothing can stop it."

"I do not quite agree with you, Tweh. God says that he will help those who help themselves. I think that we should help ourselves. This is why you contacted the Zoe and we visited him in Zorzor. It might be too late tomorrow."

"Definitely, I will not drink any country medicine or wear any rope around my waist, Lu. I don't believe in all that stuff."

"Okay, if you say so, fine. But I know that with the rope which the Zoe gave me, *I* am secure."

Tweh did not go back to the Zoe in Zorzor for any protection for himself. But he and the people in the neighborhood waited eagerly to see what would happen to Luciano Hamilton, the bright lady.

Luciano went to the Water Side General Market on a Saturday morning and dropped in the street. The bottle of palm oil which was in her market bag burst in the street when she fell. The ambulance came and rushed Luciano to the nearest hospital.

Luciano yelled, "The rope! The rope! The rope!"

She died fifteen minutes before the ambulance arrived at the hospital.

The ambulance driver and two police officers who accompanied the body to the hospital could not understand what Luciano meant when she cried out "The rope." But soon the true story concerning the rope spread all over Monrovia, especially on Ashmun Street.

The Zoe became not only the consulting witch doctor for the Tweh and Mantarda families, but for most people on Ashmun Street. Some big shots in Monrovia spent their weekends in Zorzor to consult the Zoe.

But Tweh refused to acknowledge the veracity of the Zoe in all country medicine affairs. That was his problem.

There is a Liberian saying that goes, "The last button on Joe's coat is invaluable." If all the buttons on your coat are cut except one, it is wise to take good care of the last button or else you would be left with nothing to fasten your coat. You may use a safety pin, but a safety pin looks odd on a coat.

The same is true in the case of any last child in a family. In Africa, if the last and only child is a boy, he must be able to shoulder greater responsibilities, because it is he who will perpetuate the name and image of his family. If, however, the last and only child is a girl, the family is said to be cursed by God and nature. That is, the name of the family would go into oblivion after the girl is married. The father and mother as well as the relatives would cry nearly every day because a woman simply cannot take a man's place. A boy child is preferable to a girl, and especially if that is the only child in the family.

Tweh named Lu's last child after his mother, Boryonon. The child also had to bear a Christian name, so Lucretia named Boryonon after her grandmother, Mary.

Mary Boryonon, Tweh's African and Christian names always rang a bell in the ears of her parents and relatives. She represented the old people. Mary was expected to inherit most of the characteristics of her grandmother as well as those of her great-grandmother. As the last button on her parents' coat, much was expected from Mary.

Lucretia, however, did not believe that Mary was the last child, as the witch doctor had foretold. She did all she could to get pregnant again after Mary was born, but failed.

The family doctor administered all kinds of treatments so that Lucretia would conceive. He made arrangements for Lu to take treatment in America and Europe, but to no avail. Lucretia could not even menstruate anymore, just as the Zoe said in Zorzor.

That was a great burden on Lucretia, the Mantarda and Tweh families. Lu almost worried herself to death, wishing for a boy child.

Commissioner Tweh ransacked a considerable number of young girls and women in Monrovia and throughout the country for a boy. His efforts did not materialize.

Even though Tweh and Lu were legally married in Church, he could have brought in any child, especially a boy, and his wife would not have rejected the child. Tweh could have given Lucretia a good sum of money, say five hundred dollars, so that she would forgive him for having another child out of their marriage. The boy child would have been socially accepted in the city and country; Tweh would have gotten an affidavit, legitimizing the boy.

But none of Tweh's women could get pregnant. Mary Tweh had closed the door for any more children for Tweh and Lucretia, according to the old people. Mary closed the door for all the children so that her parents would give her all the attention and care.

Chapter 8

To love a child is good. It is incumbent upon all parents and guardians to love their children and to care for them. But parents should not love their children to the point of spoiling them. Exaggerated sympathy and care should not exceed the interest of parents in training their children.

Mary Tweh almost became a spoiled child by the mother. Lucretia treated Mary like a "chicken egg," as if she would fall on the floor and break. She did not want Mary to cry for anything for a long time. And the only way a baby communicates is by crying. Some babies cry when eating. Some cry as a means of taking exercise, to exercise the throat or the sides. But Lucretia would rather die and come back before she could see Mary cry for at least two minutes.

Before Mary was two years old, the parents bought a lot on Camp Johnson Road; they built a three-bedroom house behind Monrovia College and moved there.

Lucretia contacted the Principal of Monrovia College for Mary to attend the kindergarten division of the school before she turned two years. The principal indicated that Mary was too small to absorb any lessons.

When she told Tweh of the effort she made to have Mary enrolled at Monrovia College, Tweh hired a senior student at Monrovia College to teach Mary at home. Even before Mary started to attend the kindergarten at Monrovia College, she could read and recite the alphabet very well. She could recognize and interpret pictures; she graduated from kindergarten one year before her classmates.

Commissioner Tweh also employed an elderly lady who took care of Mary, even though the mother was not working. Lucretia hardly did anything at home. She simply supervised the activities of children in the kitchen and the lady who took care of Mary. The elderly woman did all the changing of Mary's diapers, bathing and feeding.

Mary's nurse came to work earlier than 7 a.m. in order to walk the little girl to school which was within a stone's throw distance. And she was at the gate of Monrovia College at 10:25 a.m. to escort Mary back home. The first session of the kindergarten which Mary attended was out at 10:30 a.m.

The grandparents of Mary, Mr. and Mrs. Mantarda, wanted the little girl to live with them on Broad Street. Tweh and his wife could not see their way clear to have their only child live elsewhere. Mary only spent time and weekends with the grandparents and some aunts.

The parents of Tweh in New Kru Town often visited the Commissioner and his wife on Camp Johnson Road. Old lady Wesseh brought Mary and the mother coconuts, farina, palm nuts and cassava nearly every weekend.

Mary was the only "rose" in the family. And she knew that, too. She played baby by crying for anything for a long time. If she wanted anything, a new dress, for example, Mary would cry and roll herself on the floor. If Tweh did not have any money at the time, Lucretia would quickly send to her father on Broad Street; and if the grandfather had no money on hand readily, he would go into his savings account at the First National City Bank just to buy the dress.

There were some things which Mary did not really need and yet the parents bought for her. They bought her gold finger and earrings every month. She received several gold and diamond rings every birthday. Before she was twelve years of age, Mary had a whole trunk of jewels.

Her birthday celebrations took two days. All the friends of Commissioner Tweh and Lucretia came over to their house to drink, eat and dance on the eve of the birthday. And at 12 a.m., champagne bottles flowed; the parents threw a lavish dinner on the birthday for over one hundred people.

Mary was growing up as a spoiled child. Everybody in the neighborhood knew that the parents were responsible for the child being spoiled. Mary would not demean herself if visitors were around in their house. Some of the neighbors talked with Lucretia and Tweh about the behavior of the little girl.

Lucretia often told her neighbors that Mary was the baby in the family, the only child so far, so she needed extraordinary care.

Lucretia pointed out that she did not want to do anything that would hurt the feelings of her baby.

Lucretia was very unreasonable when it came to judging Mary. Whenever Mary and another girl or boy fought while playing in the yard, Lucretia would, without any thorough investigation, blame the cause of the fight on the other child. Mary was always innocent.

What a fallacy! Is there anybody who is infallible? Perhaps Lucretia refused to recognize the fact that the other children had feelings, just as Mary had. The parents of the other children were as concerned about the welfare and protection of their children. In some instances, Tweh would not apologize to the parents of the other children, or reprimand Mary in the presence of his neighbors.

The Grebo people say that one cannot categorically judge the palaver of two children; children do not know right from wrong; two children may fight now and become the best of friends again in the next fifteen minutes.

Old man Wesseh and his wife were aware of the situation involving Mary and some of the other children in the neighborhood. Every time Wesseh and his wife visited the Twehs, Mary would act unbecomingly; and as grandparents they made attempts to correct the little girl, in the presence of her parents. But Lucretia would not stand for that. And seemingly, what Lucretia said was 'the gospel' at home. She made most of the decisions, decisions which had bearings on the image of the family, especially decisions affecting the future of Mary, the only child.

Old man Wesseh could not condone that. He decided to talk with Tweh about the little girl and other matters. He diplomatically extended an invitation to Tweh and Lucretia to visit them in New Kru Town; he knew, however, that Lucretia would never visit them.

"No, old man, I will not be able to come to New Kru Town. Tweh alone can go with you. If you like, he can carry Mary along with him to visit you people. But I am not coming," Lucretia said.

"I knew, Lu, that you would not go with us to see the family in New Kru Town. I cannot remember the last day you visited us in New Kru Town, say after you and Tweh were married. However, Tweh and Mary can visit us this evening, if you will not be able to go."

"It is not that I don't want to come to see you and your wife, old man. But I am not used to going to New Kru Town.

"Is that all the reason why you will not come?"

"Yes. That's all. Don't misunderstand me, old man. I am not too proud to come to New Kru Town. But I am just not used to going there. Period. And there is no one to change my mind, either."

"No, it is not the matter of changing your mind; the issue here is purely a family affair. If we are supposed to be one family and one body, which we are, then I think that you should be able to find time to visit us one day and see how we are doing. This is why we come here often to see you, Tweh and Mary. We should be concerned about your health, whether you are sick or not. This is how we Africans should live; this is how our people have always lived."

"Yes, old man. You have a point there. But we have several categories of Africans: the western oriented Africans and the unaffected Africans or those who still believe and practice the African way of living.

"For some of us who were born in Monrovia and have been living in Monrovia all the days of our lives, we do not believe in the extended family system, which allows all the brothers, sisters, aunts, uncles and all the relatives to call on any other relative without previous notice. The category in which you and your wife fall is quite different from mine; I do not know about Tweh. For example, you can sit all night to judge woman palaver and all that stuff~ And I am not for that.... As I said earlier, Tweh can go with you to New Kru Town if he wishes. You and Mary can go; but I am not going with you to sit among the Kru people, talking their dialect; and you know that I do not understand your dialect. Everybody speaks the dialect around there."

"You can learn Kru, Lu."

"Learn what? No way, old man. I can't learn Kru."

"I do understand your problem, Lu. I would not persuade you to go to New Kru Town with me, if you do not want to go. You do not expect some of the women in New Kru Town to speak English to you if they have never learned

English. They never went to school. I happen to speak small English because I work at the dock and aboard the ships. My wife cannot speak or understand one word of English. But that does not mean that she cannot communicate with you through someone; and that does not mean that when you are around here she should not talk her dialect, the only means of communication for her. Tweh, to whom you are married, could not speak or write English; today he is a college graduate. He had to go to school and learn the language."

"Let's forget it, old man. If Lu does not want to go to New Kru Town because the people there speak Kru, I will go with you.

After all, I was living in New Kru Town when I met Lu at Daniel E. Howard before we went to Liberia College. I am a Kru and will remain one until I die," Tweh said.

Since Tweh seemed to be a bit disturbed, old man Wesseh did not want the conversation to continue any further. He advised Tweh to leave the house, for he did not want any hard feelings.

"I will dress up Mary and she will go with us to New Kru Town. I have go to visit my people," Tweh added.

"You and Mary can go. But I am not going. I told you this before," Lu replied.

Tweh hurriedly located little Mary's shoes, put them on her and changed her dress. Old man Wesseh was in the front seat of the car and Mary was in the back seat, all by herself. Old man Wesseh began to tell Tweh the main reason why he wanted to see him in New Kru Town.

"You see, Tweh, the issue between you and your wife is purely cultural conflict. I must admit that your wife, Lu, is a nice woman. She has not done anything wrong to my wife, the family and me. She always cooks for us whenever we visit you people on Camp Johnson Road. But she does not look at things the way we do. She is western by training, education and religion. She does not believe in our extended family system; and that all our relatives in the country should visit you in Monrovia. Definitely, she would not like it—not that she is bad, but because she is not used to that.

"According to your marriage, she should be the only woman for you, because you made an open declaration in church that she will be your only wife until death. Lucretia knows that the family, I mean we, the so-called country people, are not happy that you have only this little girl in the back seat. We want a son in the family. We want a son that will bear your name forever, even after your death. This is why she does not want to see you around us. She knows that we will, in one way or the other, influence you to marry another woman or have a girlfriend outside."

"I agree with you, old man. But what gets on my nerves is that she feels too superior and proud to visit you, my own people, you people that she should count before me," Tweh pointed out while steering the wheel of his car.

"Yes, you are correct. But she is your wife. You have got to be with her until death. In fact, her action does not warrant divorce, in the eyes of the law. It is not legally wrong to say that she only knows you and little Mary as her only family. You have got to take it easy.... Now, we the family in New Kru Town and Governor Woljroh are concerned about you. You must have another child besides Mary.

"It is a pity that most of your equals, Weah, Yankoon and Seleweon have grown-up boys. Oftentimes they approach me about you. They cannot talk this over with you because of your position. The Governor volunteered to give you his own daughter, Kokoday, as your girlfriend. She will live with her parents in New Kru Town and you can see her once or twice a week. She is about sixteen years old, a young girl. Her breasts have not even fallen."

"You mean this is why you came to call me?"

"Yes, Tweh. This is a serious matter. You would not know how serious it is until you meet the Governor and some people presently at my house. They are waiting for you. The Governor has told his daughter and she has agreed to be your girlfriend, just to have a boy for you. I know that your wife will never have any other child. I am sure that no one from New Kru Town will ever tell her anything about the girl."

"Okay, let's go and meet with them. But old man, you should have brought this to my attention while we were at the house; at least I would have brought with me sufficient money to entertain the people. I think I only have twenty dollars with me in my wallet."

"That is too much money, my son. We don't want any money from you. I think your Ma did buy some beer and cane juice for the people. If I am not wrong, I think she bought about three dollars worth of cane juice and a case of big club beer."

"Even though you and Ma made preparation for the gathering, I feel that I should give the people something to drink and buy their tobacco. I am not paying them, but for the sake of respect for the old people."

When Tweh drove into his father's yard in New Kru Town, everybody stood up to greet him. The Kru people had great respect for him, just as he did for them. Tweh was the only light or recognized "civilized" man among the Krus in Monrovia.

Indeed, he was embarrassed for the honor. Some of the people who stood for Tweh were by far older than he; and he felt that the honor was too much.

Speaking in Kru he said, "Please have your seats; I should have stood for **YOU**, instead. I am your servant, for you all helped to make me what *I* am today. I feel flattered by your gesture."

The council sat; and to what Tweh said, Governor Woljroh advanced a rebuttal.

"You may be correct, Commissioner Tweh. But in view of your achievement in life, you are older than all of us, especially those of us living in Monrovia. We look to you as our father for protection socially, politically, and economically. If any of us should go to court tomorrow, *I* am sure that you will be the only person to come to the rescue of that person. We know that some of us are older than you, according to chronological ages; but you are older than we, according to our life in today's modern world."

"Yes Sir, Governor. There is no need to argue. Good evening, gentlemen."

"Good evening, Commissioner Tweh," the full house replied. Everybody took his seat, ready to hear the opening remarks of the Saturday evening talk.

Before the opening statement, Mrs. Wesseh brought a plate of kola, pepper, salt and a big cup of cold water. She handed them to old man Wesseh who appropriately introduced the occasion by presenting the kola to the council.

Governor Woljroh, on behalf of the council, accepted the kola and invited members of the council to partake of the kola, urging them to contribute substantially toward the success of the gathering.

Almost in unison, the councilmen ate the kola and pepper from the plate and small bowl. They drank from the same cup; the pepper was hot.

In less than five minutes, everybody was ready to hear the nature of the council.

Chapter 9

Governor Woljroh, presiding, said, "It should not be surprising to you, Commissioner Tweh, to see that the house of your old man is full this evening. We are here because we feel that your worries are our burdens. Your happiness is ours; we should, as a people, share the burdens of one another.

"If you can recall, some of us were among those who went with your old man to talk with your parents-in-law when your wife was pregnant at the time when the two of you were still in school at Liberia College. This is the second time we are looking into your marriage palaver. You can see that we are all family people here this evening. There is no strange person among us. Feel relaxed among us because we are relaxed with you.

"I personally consider *it* an honor to be associated with you in such a matter, marriage and children. I would not feel ashamed to tell you how we (the Kru people) feel about you and children. We are aware, that you are legally married in church and that you should only marry one wife until you die or she dies. That is fine and beautiful. But I believe your wife is a bit old now to have another child; I believe that the only child you have is the little girl in your lap. We the Krus in New Kru Town are worried about a boy child for you. You must have a boy child who will bear your name. This is why we are here this evening to meet with you and hear your side of the story. What have you to say?"

"I am grateful Governor and members of the council, for the interest that you have manifested in me. It is quite true that the issue of a boy in my family is crucial, not only in my family but in the family of any married African. I am aware of it. But there is nothing I can do about it," Tweh replied.

"Gentlemen, I think that we are on the way of solving this problem. Tweh has rightfully identified the problem, agreed that it exists; only he does not know how to solve it. .. . Well, we know how to handle the problem for you, Commissioner. My wives and I have decided over the last three months to give you our third daughter for your second wife or girlfriend. Her name is Kokoday. Since you are legally married, she will live with us in New Kru Town. We will give her a separate room. And you can visit her anytime you want to," Governor Woljroh explained.

"It would be very difficult for me to do so, Governor. Suppose my wife should hear about your daughter? I personally would be in serious trouble with her. In fact, you and your wives as well as my old man, would all be in terrible conflict with Lucretia. I hope that you gentlemen will see with me."

Old man Wesseh said, 'That should not be your concern. The Governor and his wives know that you are married, and they have agreed to give you their own daughter. I am positive that no one from New Kru Town would ever tell your wife that you have another wife or girlfriend in New Kru Town."

"Your old man is correct, Commissioner. Leave everything to us. We will manage everything for you because you are our man. We will see to it that it is kept a secret from your wife," Koon assured Tweh.

"I made myself explicit to you earlier, my son. If my wives, the Kru people and I did not love you and if we did not respect you, we would not have decided to make Kokoday available to you. Don't be afraid of what your wife will do. Definitely, she cannot do anything to my family and me. She cannot sue us in court. If anything, she will sue you for adultery; and an adultery case is hard to decide in court. What is more, she will never hear of my daughter. I trust the Kru people. We are united when it comes to such a matter as this. Therefore, you should say something better to the gathering here," the Governor added.

"I would like to thank all of you for the offer; I am particularly thankful to the Governor and his wives. The gathering here this evening is an indication that we are united, that we care for one another. I do agree to have Kokoday as my girl friend, even though I have not seen her," Tweh replied.

"That is no problem, Commissioner. We will call the girl so you can see her. I am sure that she knows you; she was a small girl when you were living with your old man. We will ask her right here, whether she likes you or not," the Governor noted.

There is nothing more to be discussed. Old man Wesseh called the girl to come in. It was difficult for Kokoday to come into the house. Ladies are always shy to go among men, especially a council of men, and express themselves. But Kokoday's presence was absolutely necessary.

Her mother convinced her to go in and say a few words, to answer a few questions.

Kokoday came in and sat beside her father.

"Kokoday, we have called you here regarding what your mothers and I discussed with you earlier. This house is filled to capacity because of you. Do you know Commissioner Tweh, the man sitting at the head of the table?" the father asked.

"Yes, I know him."

"Have you seen him before?"

"Yes. I have seen him before. Isn't he old man Wesseh's son? He was living here with his father before he got married and moved to Monrovia. Right?"

"You are right, my daughter.. . do you want him to be your boyfriend?"

"Yes, Pa."

"The matter is before you now, Commissioner. This is my daughter, Kokoday. You listened to her, that she loves you. Do you love her also?"

"Yes, Governor."

"Our gathering here is not fruitless, gentlemen. Our mission is accomplished. You gentlemen listened to both Tweh and Kokoday; their responses are positive. My wives and I will entertain you people tonight. Get the billygoat and slaughter it. We will be here, playing and dancing until tomorrow morning."

The councilmen greeted the finishing comments of the Governor with a standing ovation. Old man Wesseh rounded up all the young girls and older women in the neighborhood to come over to his place and sing. Drums echoed the news of the new wife for Commissioner Tweh.

Old man Wesseh sent for more beer and cane juice for the dancers and elders. Tweh gave the old people twenty dollars for their tobacco and 'cold water.'

He asked to be excused in order to take little Mary back to his wife on Camp Johnson Road. It was quite late for Mary to be out. The elders granted him the excuse. Tweh went home and told his wife that he had to go back to New

Kru Town for a serious investigation. Lucretia told him to go with pleasure. The Tweh-Kokoday dance lingered on until broad day on Sunday. The Krus danced and made merriment.

Tweh was married for the second time. He divided his time almost equally between Lucretia and Kokoday. He had to please both of his women. If Tweh was not out of Monrovia on official business, he spent at least two to four days in New Kru Town. He told Lucretia that he had to be either in Gbarnga or Tchien for an investigation. His game worked out very well. Lucretia never met or heard of Kokoday.

Lucretia could not have suspected Tweh of having another wife elsewhere because his salary was not affected. Tweh earned some extra money by virtue of his position as Provincial Commissioner and he used this extra money to support Kokoday and other girlfriends.

Kokoday and Tweh were together for over eight years; unfortunately, she never got pregnant. She visited all the gynecologists in Monrovia in order to get pregnant. No way.

The doctors told Tweh and Kokoday that she had a small womb; pregnancy was almost impossible unless she underwent a major operation out of Liberia.

The operation was estimated to cost no less than $2700, not to mention the fare for her round trip to either Europe or America.

The father of Kokoday, old man Wesseh and other members of Tweh's immediate family did not believe what the gynecologists said; instead, they believed what the Zoe said in Zorzor, that Tweh would never have any child after Mary.

Tweh had nothing to do or say about the findings of the Zoe; he knew that nothing was wrong with him; he was not impotent. Lucretia had forgotten by now all about having a baby. She was too old to conceive. There came a time when Tweh, too, forgot about having a baby.

84

Mary Tweh was growing very fast. She was attending the College of West Africa, a Methodist high school in Monrovia. She was about thirteen years old, attending the junior high division of the school.

It was at the close of September that year when the Government of Liberia received an invitation for the Secretary of the Interior to attend a conference of Interior Secretaries from some one hundred countries, scheduled to take place in Cairo, Egypt. The Liberian Interior Secretary was at the time out of the country on a health trip to West Germany; the president designated Commissioner Tweh to represent the Government of Liberia at the international conference, which was to last for six weeks.

The trip to Egypt was one of the most prestigious to be attended by Tweh. He was going to the conference as Ambassador of Liberia. That was another noticeable achievement on the part of Tweh.

The Kru people were extremely happy and proud about his selection. The Kru Goodwill Organization in New Kru, Logan and Clara Towns chartered three buses to convey well wishers to Roberts International Airport, and see Commissioner Tweh off.

Lucretia, Mary and Tweh rode with Tweh's driver to the airport. Lucretia told Tweh on their way to Roberts Field that she was quite embarrassed for what she termed "the noise" of the Kru people. She did not like the idea of a whole lot of people coming to see her husband off.

Tweh paid no attention to Lucretia. He was with his people, and that was very important to Tweh; the idea that over fifty people risked their lives to see him off. Tweh was like a Paramount Chief of the Kru people.

The Krus prayed for God's blessing and protection upon Tweh before he left for Cairo. He really needed prayers. That was the last time they would ever see him. Tweh's flight took off from Roberts Field during the early hours of the morning; and the buses got to Monrovia about 11:45 a.m.

The plane was caught in a tumultuous storm off the coast of Egypt; the storm overpowered the plane and it burst into flames in midair. There were no survivors. All one hundred and fifty passengers, mostly delegates to the conference and the six crew members, were burned to ashes.

The news concerning the tragedy came on the air at 5:15 p.m. The radio station quoted the flight number of Tweh's plane.

What broke out in New Kru Town and Monrovia was like a war. The irreparable loss was too great to sustain.

Commissioner Tweh died in a plane crash! Unbelievable! Why did he have to die at this time? Did Tweh have any boy child by his wedded wife? No. He had any permanent girlfriends outside? Yes. He had any boy by any of his girlfriends? No. What bad luck in the Tweh family! These were some of the questions discussed by mourners when the news broke out in Monrovia and in Liberia.

The Government of Liberia arranged a Requiem Mass at the Centennial Memorial Pavilion, for the peaceful repose of Tweh's soul.

The Krus staged a false burial in memory of Commissioner Tweh, for one long week both in Monrovia and Sasstown.

Tweh died intestate; his rubber farm in Kakata was not fully developed. Mary was still in school, and Lucretia was not working. She had no other income. The responsibility of Mary's education rested on her shoulders.

There was no time for Mary to play baby anymore. "The Zoe in Zorzor told nothing but the truth," Lucretia shouted. "But we did not believe him. It is too late! My husband is gone, gone to the great beyond! Who will help me with this child?"

Sure enough, it was late.

To every problem there should be a solution.

Chapter 10

Life devoid of experience is not complete. A person's life is the sum total of all of his experiences; life experience is like an institution of higher learning.

Mary Tweh bought her own love experiences before she was promoted to the third year class at the College of West Africa (CWA).

Experience bought should stay within our skulls forever for future reference; secondhand experience is, to some degree, alienated.

Mary was a beautiful girl; she was attractive not only to her classmates, but to the staff and faculty of her school. She had brown skin, long fingers and big eyes. Her black hair was shoulder length. Her silver, gold and diamond jewelry added tempting beauty to her overall 5'11" personality with black gums, her teeth flashed like lightning.

A true representation of God's finest creation, Mary Tweh was a complete temptation to anybody who saw her.

Above all, she was polite to everybody in school. Her attitude toward life and people changed, following the death of her father and grandfather. She could no longer ride under the protective umbrella of Commissioner Tweh or Hon. Mantarda. She had to face the reality of life that you have to be what you are, not the image of someone else. It is not good to depend upon the achievements of your parents or grandparents.

Old lady Lucretia sold the car that Tweh had bought before his death. The mother needed every cent to support Mary and herself; and therefore Mary walked to and from school every morning and afternoon. One of Mary's classmates, Emmanuella S. James Tesela Dennis, sometimes offered her a lift.

James was the oldest of his brothers and sisters, some of whom were also attending CWA as well as B. W. Harris. As the oldest brother, James rode with the driver in the front seat. Therefore it was easy for James to see Mary while she was walking to school, on the sidewalk.

Most of the time as they drove by C. D. B. King Elementary School, James would spy Mary afar in her blue and white uniform.

"Look, driver, stop for that girl. She is going to the same school as me; we are classmates. Give her a lift," James would tell the driver.

The driver would stop for Mary; and without saying a word, she would enter on James's side and sit next to him in the front seat.

"Good morning, everybody."

"Good morning, Mary. How are you today?" James asked.

"I am doing fine, except that I was walking to school this morning and you bless my soul."

"Don't mention."

James developed latent interest in Mary, as time went by; even the brothers and sisters as well as the driver began to manifest interest in Mary. The lifts were so frequent that Mary subconsciously waited for James at the Monrovia

College gate, just in front of her house. The driver no longer had to wait for James to instruct him to stop for Mary. It was almost automatic; he would simply park the car along Camp Johnson Road for Mary to come in. Such was the beginning and root of the friendship between James and Mary Tweh.

James without delay launched a romantic campaign to win the love of Mary, through her friend, Theresa, also a student at CWA. The campaign would not have been effective had it not been for the kindness which James and the driver showed. Love blended with genuine kindness moves faster than lip-service love. Generally, a woman will not forget you easily if you are kind to her during your romantic games.

James told Theresa that he was interested in Mary, but he did not know how to go about reaching her

"Theresa, I like your friend, Mary Tweh. But I am shy to tell her. Can you help me talk to her, since the two of you are friends?" James inquired.

"Yes, James. Mary is my intimate friend; we are thick buddies. She might agree if I tell her. But she is very unpredictable. And love relations are personal matters. I would not like to influence her decision, because she will solely be involved. I would suggest that you sit with us at our table in the cafeteria for coffee, and from there you can attack. I will be around, as if I do not know what is going one," Theresa said.

"I will do exactly as you said. Theresa. I will take the two of you to the cafeteria tomorrow, and I will try to talk to her. If she prefers writing, I can write her a beautiful letter. . . but it is old-fashioned these days to write to a girl. Boys and girls from the old school wrote love letters. We modern boys and girls sit and talk things over while drinking or partying."

"That is true, James. There is no need writing. Mary is my friend; I can talk to her."

The James-Theresa strategy worked. Theresa delayed Mary in the corridor of the school for a few minutes, during recess, waiting for James.

"Do you have any money to go to the cafeteria today, Mary?" asked Theresa.

"No, I have no money today. Have you any money?"

"Yes. But it is not sufficient for both of us. We can only buy two pieces of cornbread. We need coke or something to drink," Theresa replied.

By that time James came down the hall, running and out of breath.

"Hello, girls. How are you today?"

"We are trying our best to survive. We were just talking about going to the cafeteria," Theresa said.

"Shall we go?"

"We do not have sufficient money, James."

"That is no problem, Theresa. I can treat the two of you."

Mary looked at Theresa while Theresa looked at Mary, as if asking the opinion of each other.

"Let's go, Mary. The gentleman has volunteered to treat us this morning. Food is a blessing and we are not turning it down, especially since we have no money today," Theresa said.

"Okay, let's go," Mary agreed.

James felt like a king, just to think that Mary had agreed to eat with him at the same table. He was more than happy to sponsor the cafeteria treat.

The cafeteria was almost jammed to capacity when they arrived. Most boys and girls were already eating. Some students were still standing in line, waiting to be served.

"I think we should eat *fufu* and soup," James suggested.

"That would be okay with us," Theresa replied. The two girls settled in the corner of the cafeteria. James quickly placed in the order for *fufu* and soup and all the ingredients that go with fufu—mashed okra, hot pepper and benny-seeds.

James had to nail the nail real hard on the head of Mary in order to win her love. First impression counts.

"What do you think about the social life at CWA, Mary?" James asked.

"Well, I would not say anything much about the social life here on campus. Theresa would be the better person to ask. For one thing, I do not go out too much. The last time I went out was when Theresa and her boyfriend, Tommy, took me to a dance at the Pavilion. The second time this year Tommy and Theresa took me to the Easter dance. That's all I can say."

"Why don't you like to go out?" Is it that you do not have a boyfriend? Or is it that you do not like the boys at CWA?"

"Answering the first question, no. I don't have any boyfriend. The second question, yes. I like the boys here. Maybe I have not met the right one. Those who asked me so far are not up to expectations.

"What do you mean they are not up to expectations?" asked Theresa.

"I mean they are not thinking in the same direction as I do. They are not aggressive; they tend to put emphasis on their classroom achievements only—grades and that's all. There is more to life than scoring good grades in school, because after school you go into the world. And almost ninety percent of what we learn in school cannot be related to the things we do in life. Right?"

"That is true, Mary. For example, my younger brother in the tenth grade here on campus does not know how to approach any girl or any boy. He cannot make good conversation. All he does is to study his lessons, come to school and go on errands for our parents. He is socially dead. He

92

does not even know the names of some of his classmates, especially girls. That is a shame on his part. And he is not the only one like that," added James.

"That is just exactly what I am saying, that some of the boys are not socially inclined. I must say here however, that some boys here at CWA are social giants. They socialize; they can discuss any topic with you, be it politics, economics, religion, diplomacy, or what have you," Mary said.

"What is happening this weekend? Maybe we could go out, that is, if that will meet the approval of Theresa and her boyfriend, Tommy." James changed the course of the conversation, looking in the eye of Mary.

"I think the Monrovia Rotary Club is having a ball this Saturday, at the Ducor Intercontinental Hotel," Theresa said.

"That is correct, Theresa. I almost forgot. I am a member of the Rotary Club and I should be at the ball. Could we go that day?"

"Yes, James. But I will have to discuss this with my boyfriend. I will have to tell Tommy in advance, or else he would not go. He likes procedure and protocol."

"I don't think anything is wrong with that. You have got to plan in advance; planning is one of the essential elements of life," James observed.

"Yes, James. But when you do it to the extreme, then it bothers me. Tommy is too strict."

"Is he member of the Rotary Club, Theresa?"

"No. If he were a member, you would have seen him at Rotary meetings."

"I see. . . what about you, Mary? Will you go?"

"If Theresa and her boyfriend will go, then I will go. You know I can't go alone."

"I can take you out that day; would that be okay?"

93

"No. I told you earlier that Theresa and her boyfriend, Tommy, will take me out. I do appreciate your invitation. Usually, my mother allows me to go out with Theresa and Tommy. Definitely, she would not like the idea that I go out with you. In the first place, she does not know you; she knows that I have no boyfriend. How can I tell her that I am going out with you?"

"You have a point there. In any case, I would like you all to go with me to the ball."

"No sweat," Theresa concluded.

Chapter 11

Recess was over for over fifteen minutes. The cafeteria date was tentative, yet it had impact on Mary. She was highly impressed with James. Being a member of the Rotary Club while still in high school meant a lot. That was a sign of positive leadership, initiative, manhood and social acceptance.

Many more thoughts came to Mary's mind. She thought about the Rotary dance, with James as the sponsor. She knew that the number was square, two boys and two girls. She was aware that a girl must dance with a boy, and that Theresa was to be with her boyfriend, Tommy. She was, of course, to be left in the hungry and ravaging hands of James.

Women generally know if you are chasing them. They are smart, smarter than men when it comes to romantic affairs.

When school was over, Mary invited Theresa to her house, for lunch. James told the driver to drop the two girls on Camp Johnson Road; but the girls told James that they would be strolling home.

James gestured at Theresa, reminding her to represent his interest to Theresa.

Mary and Theresa caught James's eyes. Mary smiled. The smile of Mary was inviting; it seemed to James to be telling him, "Here I am, take me over; I am at your disposal."

"Theresa, what do you think James is after?" Mary asked.

"Mary," Theresa replied, "you are not a child. You should know if a boy is interested in you or not. Actions speak louder than words. Don't you know that, Mary?"

"Yes. This is why I am posing the question. I know that he is interested in me. But he has not told me anything. Maybe he has expressed his desire to you."

"Yes. He told me, I think two days ago. But I told him to approach you, since in fact, you will be directly involved.. I will not be around; and he is going about it diplomatically. What do you think of James, Mary?"

"I should ask you, Theresa, because he is approaching me through you. Except that all of us are classmates, I know nothing about James. I casually know all of his brothers and sisters at B. W. Harris School and CWA; they always bring me to school. And that's all. Nothing more."

"Why do you think he always offers you a lift? He admires you. James is deadly in love with you. He told me this."

"Well, I hope that he is not using his father's car to entice me. Material things don't move me. While it is true that we cannot do without material things, they do not make me lose my sense of judgment. He seems to have nice ways; I don't know for sure."

Mary and Theresa were so inextricably involved in their conversation that they arrived home late; they took about forty-five minutes to go from CWA to Camp Johnson Road. Normally, it took Mary fifteen minutes. Mary's mother was impatient waiting for her baby to arrive from school.

"What has happened to you today, baby?" old lady Lu asked.

"Nothing, Ma. Theresa and I were just walking slowly because the sun is burning hot."

"Oh, I see. . . have a seat, Theresa. I have not seen you for long time. Where have you been?"

"I am here, Ma. Lessons are rough these days. All the teachers are real tough these days; this is why I haven't visited Mary often in recent weeks."

"That is good, little girl. It is good to have you girls busy with school assignments. It keeps you out of trouble. Mary, get two spoons and bring the food to the table. I know you girls are hungry," old lady Lu said while she reclined in her antique chair.

As usual, old lady Lu started to advise the girls how to study harder in school.

"My children, I want the two of you to study together. You should forget about man palaver now. I know these Monrovia boys very well. They like to spoil young girls in town."

"Ma, we will try our best in school. Your daughter, Mary, is very serious in school. You can see that in her report card," Theresa said.

"Yes, I know that Mary's grades are good. One of your teachers met me at the General Market yesterday and told me the same thing. But having good grades in school doesn't mean everything. You can have good grades and be pregnant in a minute. I know what I am talking about. I am speaking from experience.

"I was like you when my husband, I mean Mary's father, impregnated me. We didn't know any better during those days. But my old man, 'peace be to his ashes,' made Tweh marry me immediately. I would have graduated from old Liberia College, but I could not because I was pregnant. Not that I was not doing well in school. And in those days if a girl is pregnant while in school, she is finished. She would not go to any other school. Now, here I am. Poor me. No Pa, no

Ma, no husband. If Mary should get pregnant in school, how would I manage with the mother and the child?"

"Ma, Mary will not get pregnant. She and I are always together. ... . Liberia, as you know, is changing very fast. Today we have women secretaries, lawyers, professors, ambassadors and engineers. The competition between men and women is great, and will be greater in the years ahead. Therefore, we will do all we can to avoid pregnancy," Theresa assured Lu.

Mary and Theresa did not eat their lunch in peace; Lu was on their tail, advising them what to do and what not to do. Theresa wanted to stay a little longer, to chat with Mary before going home. But she left immediately when they finished eating.

Tommy consented to go to the Rotary dance with James, Mary and his girlfriend. Tommy and Theresa went to old lady Lu to ask her permission for Mary to go to the ball with them.

Lu told Tommy and Theresa, "I have no objection for Mary to go out on weekends. But I don't want anyone to fool her. She is welcome to go with you and Theresa, Tommy."

The date of the Rotary ball arrived. Mary selected one of her best dresses for the night. She perfumed and powdered herself ten minutes before James drove in old lady Lu's yard with Theresa and Tommy in the back seat.

James tapped the horn of the car to signal Mary that all was set to go. Theresa jumped out from the back seat to formally tell old lady Lu that they were ready to leave for the Ducor Hotel.

"Mary, we are ready now to go," Theresa shouted.

"Yes. I think that Mary is in her room. She has been ready ever since. Mary, Theresa is here now for the dance. Are you ready to go?" Lu asked.

"Yes, Ma. I am ready. I'll be there in a minute... Hi, Theresa. Where is Tommy?" Mary asked.

"He is waiting in the car."

"Okay, Ma. We are gone," Mary said.

The old lady kissed Mary on the jaw. The two girls left in high spirits.

Theresa took her seat in the back; Mary sat in the front seat with James at the wheel.

"Hello, gentlemen," Mary greeted James and Tommy.

"We are trying," James replied.

The aroma of Mary's perfume took complete control of the whole car; a passer-by could have smelled the perfume, with the windows of the car down. Her gorgeous dress was fantastic; her suspended gold earrings were as wide as a bold American dollar. She had on two diamond rings that night. James had an expensive date to contend with that night.

The dance started at 9 p.m., but James and his guests arrived at the Ducor Hotel at 10:30 p.m. The president of the Rotary Club had made his opening remarks; dinner was being served while some people were dancing. The music of the Bouncers, one of the leading dance bands in Monrovia, was barking on the stage. Everyone at the dance was entitled to a free drink and meal.

James and his friends occupied one table; they ordered their free drinks and had their dinner together. The romantic equation was balanced, a boy to a girl. The message was loud and clear—you are for me and I am for you.

The table at which Mary and her friends sat was like a magnet, drawing the attention of both men and women. Their group was the central attraction. Mary was well-dressed dressed like a bitch. She knew that, too.

James was very proud of his association with Mary Tweh. Well-known personalities in Monrovia surged to their table to ask Mary Tweh for a dance. Before she left her seat to dance with anyone, she obtained the permission of James.

James and Mary were not only in love at the dance; they made their love affair public to the elite and members of the semi-middle class in Monrovia. The need did not exist for James to tell Mary, "I love you."

Sometimes it is not necessary to tell a girl that you love her; the occasion speaks for itself.

Mary had to give in, as James was pumping her mouth with sentimental kisses, on the dance floor.

She told James while kissing, "All you have to do is to write my mother and tell her that you are my boyfriend; you can ask her, for the sake of respect."

"I will surely write her a decent letter," James replied. Theresa and Tommy who were now pros in their love affair, noticed that Mary and James were in real action on the floor. They were enjoying themselves.

"We brought Mary to the pool of love; now she is swimming, as if she is on cloud nine. I hope that she knows what she is doing," Theresa whispered to Tommy.

"Yes. Let the girl enjoy herself. That's life. We have to live but once," Tommy observed.

The dance was not over until 7 a.m. James took Mary home first before he dropped Theresa and Tommy to their respective homes.

"How are you doing, children? I hope that the dance was okay," old lady Lu remarked.

"It was all right, Ma. We just left the Ducor Hotel to bring Mary home," Tommy said.

"We see you, Ma.. . bye now, Mary," Theresa said.

"Okay, I see you all," Mary replied.

Mary's outlook on life was changed. She was not only a high school girl, but a girl deadly in love. She was very lively, following the Rotary dance.

Mary and James were always together, eating together in the cafeteria, riding together to and from school, even though he had not yet made their love affair official to Mary's mother.

He wrote Lucretia, registering his intention toward Mary. He gave the letter to his younger brother, Josiah, who delivered the letter to the old lady after school.

"Who wrote this letter, young man?" Lu asked.

"That's my brother, Emmanuella James Dennis."

"Emmanuella Dennis? And what he wants."

"I don't know, Ma. He simply gave me the letter for you."

"Okay. Thanks for the letter... . Mary, bring my glasses and let me read this letter; I don't know what's in it."

"Yes, Ma, where are the glasses?"

"My God! You don't know where my reading glasses are?"

"Oh, I see them, Ma. They are in the small basket." Mary handed the glasses to her Ma and ran in her room to eat her lunch. She knew the contents of the letter and therefore she did not want to be on the scene.

Old lady Lu wiped the kitchen knife with her apron and tore the envelope. She went near the window for the penetrating light. Peering with her eyes over the reading glasses, the old lady carefully read the letter. It took her about twenty-five minutes to read the letter.

"Mary, come here quick," she called.

"Yes, Ma. Why are you calling me?"

"I say come here quick and have your seat right in front of me. Let me ask you some questions. Do you know one Emmanuella Dennis?"

"Yes."

"Where is he from? Who is he?"

"He is from Monrovia, son of Senator Dennis of Montserrado County, and a student at CWA."

"So he is in the same school you are attending?"

"Yes. We are classmates"

"You mean Senator Dennis who has about fifteen houses in Sinkor and the big rubber farm near Firestone Plantations?"

"Yes. That's his son. His uncle is the Liberian Ambassador at the Court of St. James; I think two years ago he was the Liberian Ambassador in Washington D.C."

"Oh, I see. He comes from good family. But that is not enough. He is asking me for you to be his girlfriend. Is that your man already?"

"No, Ma. He told me in school the other day and I explained to him that I could not say anything until he got in touch with you. He is not my man."

"Thank you, baby. God bless your heart. I just wanted to know how far he has gone with you. I don't trust these boys in town.... Now, Mary, you are a big girl in school. You should know right from wrong, now that a boy is writing me for you. You know that I will soon die; and I want you to marry a good man, I mean a man that will have children. I mean a productive man."

"Ma, James does not say that he wants to marry me. We could, during the course of our love affair, decide to get married. I do not know his ways and be does not know my ways. How can you say that you want a productive man to marry me?"

"What are you telling me, Mary? You think that I don't know what I am saying?"

"No, I did not say so. I am simply saying that what James is proposing is quite different from marriage. You are talking

102

about marriage and he is speaking about boyfriend-girlfriend relations. These are two different things."

"Okay, Mary. I agree. What are you saying?"

"Well, Ma, I don't have much to say. It is up to you." "I have just told you my position. I agree. What else you want me to say, Mary?"

"Okay, Ma. If you say so, I agree also. You know that I can't make the decision on my own."

"But if you see James in school tomorrow, tell him that I would like to see his 'eyeballs.' I do not want anybody to fool around with my only child on earth. I know what my husband and I went through for children; **so,** tell him to come over and see me in person."

"Yes, Ma. I will deliver your message tomorrow."

Chapter 12

James could not wait to hear from Mary the next morning. When the driver stopped for Mary near Monrovia College gate, James quickly opened the door for Mary to come in.

"Hi, Mary. What is the reaction of your old lady?" he asked.

"Well, she read the letter and asked me a whole lot of questions about you. I told her that we are classmates and that I know you very well. But she would like to see you in person, to talk with you."

"Really? She wants to see me in person?"

"Yes. She wants to see you."

"When?"

"Today, tomorrow, anytime you will be available."

"I will be a man and meet with her today, after school. She cannot eat me like a lion. I am a man."

"No, she will not do anything to you, James. She just wants to make sure that she knows you in person, and that your intentions are good. That's all."

James told Theresa in school about the latest development so far. As the mediator, Theresa expressed a few words of encouragement and advice to James.

"James, you are already in the water. You have to swim or else the current will drag you down the stream. You cannot be afraid of the cold if you are already in the water. Keep on pushing.

One thing I will tell you is to take good care of Mary. She is my friend. I will also tell her to be nice to you. After all, we are classmates."

"I will do my best to take good care of Mary, Theresa. But she should do likewise. If she is nice to me, I will do my very best to make her happy. Definitely, I will stop by her house immediately after school today to see her mother."

"Yes. Be a man and stop by the house. I know she can't reject you.,'

James kept the after-school appointment. Instead of going home, he drove on Camp Johnson Road with Mary, to see old lady Lucretia.

She was sitting down, smoking her black pipe.

"Hello, young man. Are you James?" she asked.

"Yes, Ma. Good afternoon."

"Good afternoon, and have your seat."

"Thank you."

"I got your letter yesterday and I thought to talk with you. You see, when I read your letter, I did not know you. I know your father very well. I even knew your grandfather. Well, my son, I personally have nothing to say about you and Mary. You saw Mary in school and you like her. I am the mother and I cannot fall in love with her. It has to be someone like you. If she likes you, beautiful.

"The only thing I told her yesterday is that I do not want anybody to fool her. I know that you would not do it, judging from your background. You are from a good family, not only in Monrovia but in the country. I would not have agreed if you were one of those irresponsible boys in Monrovia. I mean boys who have got no future. You are welcome here anytime. Maybe you will be my son-in-law in the future. Who knows?"

James said, "I thank you very much, Ma, for your motherly advice. I would not say anything much about myself. If I wanted to make a fool out of Mary, I would not have written you, to make our relations official. I don't like back-door operations. I like to do my thing the right way. At least that's what my father has taught us. I will tell my old man about you and Mary. Perhaps he will come here one day to see you. My mother will also be happy if I tell her about Mary."

"God bless you, my son. I will be praying for you and Mary, God bless your little heart."

"Thank you very much, Ma. I see you later. I see you in school tomorrow, Mary."

"Bye, bye, James," Mary replied.

James called a taxi cab and went home, happy. He narrated the story to all his sisters and brothers and they were happy for the good news. They all liked Mary very much.

Later in the evening, James told his father and mother about Mary. The parents were also pleased about the romantic progress of their oldest son. James told his parents that having an ideal girlfriend was indicative of his maturity, sense of purpose, and willingness to assume responsibility.

Mary and James became full-time lovers. The first three months of their association was smooth. No problems. They were sweet, young, and inexperienced lovers. The present was bright; everything was going according to plan. No one knew the future.

But lovers have got to encounter rough days. There are times when lovers have got to disagree in order to agree on a point. Things must have their ups and downs. As human beings, lovers are bound to wrong one another. They must, by the same token, be willing to accept any wrong or mistake, if they want their relations to continue. This is where problems sometimes come about. Some people do not want to admit their own mistakes.

James was guilty of this. He was very dictatorial in some of his approaches to Mary. He felt superior, sophisticated and better than Mary. He would never apologize for anything he did wrong; and he did not care whether Mary's feelings were hurt.

Social superiority has got no place in the garden of love. You have got to take the person as he or she is, regardless of social attachments.

Mary was very disappointed in James. But she did not discuss his attitude with her mother. The mother had high regard for James. Instead, Mary complained to Theresa and Tommy. Tommy and Theresa tried to talk with James, but he would not listen; James felt he was always right. James was wearing the fool's hat.

Mary's complaint emanated from the confusion that James caused at a school dance.

Theresa and Tommy were not at this dance. They went to Buchanan to spend the weekend with some friends working for Lamco in Buchanan, some eighty miles southeast of Monrovia.

James had four girlfriends at the same dance, besides Mary. It was quite embarrassing, indeed. He decided to act drunk, even though he was sober.

Mary did not know the four girls. But they knew that Mary was the ideal girlfriend.

Three of the girls were attending Booker Washington Institute (BWI), a trade and industrial institution in Kakata, forty miles east of Monrovia; and the other girl was a student at St. Theresa Convent.

They all met at the dance and decided to embarrass James and harass Mary that night. They would come up to James and Mary's table and ask James to dance with them.

This was very unusual. Generally, boys do the asking at a dance, and not girls. Mary was curious to know what was going on. She told James not to dance with any of the girls anymore, because he was not the only boy at the dance. James's countenance changed; he did not want to obey Mary and yet he could not say a word.

The girls began to use sarcastic remarks.

"James is our boyfriend. All of us will dance with him tonight; he is not married to anybody here."

James and Mary heard the girls' remarks. Tension was mounting very fast. Mary's Kru blood was boiling. She was furious. She wanted to talk to the girls in strong terms; but she composed herself. It was not proper in public, especially at a school dance.

Mary became more and more jealous; love without jealousy is no love. James realized that Mary was going to react bitterly; and therefore he began to act drunk and unbecoming. James took the wrong course. Instead of staying, Mary decided that they leave and go home.

"Okay, James, let's go home. I think that you are a bit tired tonight," Mary said.

"Look, Mary, you are not here to control me. I am not married to you. I am free like the bird flying the heavens. Are you the one to tell me to go home? You are not the one. I am well known in Monrovia. Why are you harassing me? A country girl like you?" James shouted.

"1 am sorry, James, if I annoy you. I thought that I was seeking your interest, since you seem tired."

"You don't have to seek my interest. I can seek my own interest. If I am tired, I will go home. 'If you are tired, my driver will take you home. But I am not going home now."

"James, you have it all wrong. You brought me out. I did not come here by myself. I cannot leave you here and go home. You should know better than that. What will I tell my mother? That you are still at the dance and I am gone home? I am talking about social ethics, James."

"You want to teach me social ethics, Mary? No way. You have yet to learn what we call social ethics in Monrovia. And I should teach you, 'cause you are coming from the bush. Your name alone, Tweh, is synonymous with bush and jungle."

"I am sorry, James. I did not mean to say anything to hurt your feelings."

James raised his voice so loud that plenty of people came around to see what was going wrong. Mary was ashamed of herself. She asked one of her friends to take her home.

"Yes, go home. James will be here with us. He is not your husband. We are all loving him," one of James's girl-friends said.

"I am not speaking to you, please. I am treating with James, not you. You can be his girlfriend. But I am not speaking to you," Mary replied.

"Go home, Mary. If you think that you are the so-called ideal girlfriend~ we will see the end tonight. But we are tell-ing you that James is not going with you tonight," one of the girls interrupted.

"I need not argue with you or James at this time of the night. I am not used to quarreling with people, especially at this public place. I see you all." Mary left.

James and his four girlfriends remained at the dance. They made fun of Mary after she had gone.

Some of Mary's friends at the dance told her the rest of the story the next day. James had been a flamboyant playboy. Big mouth. Big cars. Big money. Plenty women. That's all.

First fool is not a fool; second fool is a fool. There is truism in the statement above.

We have got to make mistakes in life. If, for any reasons, you made the first mistake, we can excuse you. But if you repeat the same mistake over and over, then you are at fault; we may not even term your mistake a mistake, rather a habit.

Habits are hard to break.

Mary Tweh did not want to make any mistake if she met another boy; she wanted to avoid having a long list of boy-friends before marriage.

From the behavior of James, Mary Tweh learned her lesson well in love matters. She tried to learn and under-stand the behavior of men, chasing men, men who run after women for the fun of it. I mean men who are not satisfied with one woman. We have lot of those men around.

There are also some women who cannot be satisfied with one man. The case is not only against men. Women are in the same boat as men.

Some men, I mean city men, take popularity to be an excuse for promiscuous sexual fantasy. They boast of plenty and well-to-do women; they tend to close their eyes to morality.

Ironically, women admire popular men. Having plenty of girlfriends and dates at the same time is considered as a life-style, enjoyment of life, and social acceptance. They preach a new morality.

Mary Tweh still had faith in human nature; she did not assume that the attitudes of James were necessarily those of other men. That John Brown was not faithful to Eliza Jones

110

does not necessarily mean that all men are not faithful to their women, and vice versa.

Mary could still fall in love with another boy and treat him for what he was, without letting her experience with James, the playboy, sour her judgment. But she had loved James a lot; this is why she was hurt.

The one whom you love so dearly may not have time for you. Disappointment. Heartbreak? Mental derangement? Suicide? Do all these help the situation? The answer to this question, of course, is no. One must face any situation as it comes. Have courage.

Mary Tweh faced her disappointment with fortitude. She talked it over with her intimate friends, Tommy and Theresa. It is good to ventilate your sorrow by confiding in someone in whom you have confidence and trust. Better yet, take your problems to God, if you are a believer. Talk to your Nyswa, or God.

If you tell your problems to your friend, he or she might narrate similar stories, perhaps worse stories, to you. Your friends could help you, and tomorrow, you may be of help to them. This is a reciprocal world.

Tommy assumed the role of a true and genuine friend. He invited Mary and some friends to his Sinker apartment for a "friendly drink." He and Theresa wanted to talk with Mary Tweh as if she were their own sister. Either of them could have been in the same shoes as Mary, grieving over disappointment.

He went over to Mary's house and told Mrs. Lucretia Tweh about the drink. The old lady granted Mary permission to go to Tommy's house.

Chapter 13

It was on a Saturday night. Mary took a taxi cab to Sinkor, suburban Monrovia. Not many people were there at Tommy's apartment. There were about five boys and seven girls, all of whom Tommy considered as members of their "inner group."

Tommy was playing popular African and western music. Big bottles of club beer were lined up on the table like Vietnam soldiers. Everybody was enjoying himself, drinking beer, whisky, gin, brandy, and all types of wine. You name it. There was a spirit of camaraderie.

Introducing the occasion, Tommy said, "Ladies and gentlemen:

Our gathering here this evening is significant. Significant, because this occasion concerns not only a friend, but an intimate friend and sister. You all are aware of the situation between Mary Tweh and James Dennis. Even though their love affair is absolutely private, I think you and I should be as concerned as Mary is. Not because Mary will not have another boyfriend, but because she is hurt. I have been closely following the love relations between Mary and James. It was Theresa who engineered their coming together. And this is how I came in. Knowing the facts as I do, I think James did not treat Mary right. Mary is hurt. She is worrying over it, because she is still in love with James. That is affecting Mary's grades in school; her grades are diminishing very fast. And you all know that she is a clever girl.

"Some of you may say that I should have invited James here tonight. But that would not have helped the situation. Several times, Theresa and I tried to talk with James and he would not listen.

"The issue here is that I would like Mary to forget the past and look to the future. We do know the past, not the future. We can only try to predict the future. Maybe the future will be brighter for Mary. She might get a better boyfriend than James. This is why Theresa and I called you here tonight, for a drink. I feel that Mary should forget what has happened."

Responding, Mary said, "I feel so proud and happy that Tommy and Theresa are having this drink for me. I consider this an honor. They are my true friends; they care for me like my mother. All of you here, my friends, care for me also, for which I am also grateful. James and I have known one another for over six months. I mean loving, because before that we were classmates. He was my first boyfriend, and I gave him my whole heart. I used to love him. Even now, I still love him. But he has no time for me. He ridicules me in school, among my friends and classmates. I have decided to forget him, erase him completely from my mind. I don't ride with him anymore to school. I highly appreciate the kind gesture of Tommy and Theresa, for the drink tonight. Now I know who my real friends are, as of tonight."

"Does your mother know what is going on between you and James?" Theresa asked.

"No, she does not know. She however, noticed that something is going wrong, because James does not pick me up in the morning anymore. He does not visit me anymore at the house. When Ma asked me about James, I simply told her that James and I were not on good terms. I did not explain anything to her in detail. But she likes James a lot. She has high regards for him."

'Well, Mary, all of us here have our love stories. If I tell you the stories of my first girlfriend before I met Theresa, you would be shocked. I was like a crazy man in Monrovia. I used to love her too much. And she knew that, too. But she had time for other men, I mean 'big shots' in Monrovia. Some of her men almost put me in jail.

"Today, the story is different. I am happy with Theresa; we love one another. She has not done anything to me to warrant separation or heartbreak. At least I am trying my best to make her happy. I don't have any other girlfriend besides Theresa. What I am saying here is, you should be happy with us, as friends and equals. Maybe James will realize his mistake and come back to you. It is never too late to forgive," Tommy concluded.

The get-together was like a birthday party. The music from Tommy's apartment invited more boys and girls to come in. His third floor apartment was a full-house.

Those who came in later did not know the reason for the drink. Tommy did not explain anything to them. He gave them drinks and they joined the group to dance and pass the night.

One of the boys who came in later, Lysander Dormahnus Curtis, was advancing on Mary very fast. Once he discovered that Mary bad no boyfriend at the party, Lysander wanted to make good use of the opportunity. He danced several records with her, talking persuasively.

Mary was not thinking about love matters. She was just smiling, and dancing. A circumstantial love affair is as baseless and shaky as the love influenced by parents and guardians.

Mary told Lysander on the dance floor that she was not interested in anybody at the time. She just wanted to socialize and meet different people. But she did not want to hurt his feelings or anyone else's. Mary danced with all the boys at the drink that night. When she felt sleepy, she asked Tommy to take her home. It was late in the morning, about 2 a.m.

The rest of the boys and girls were not sleepy. To them the night was still young. Some of them took taxi cabs from Sinkor to the Holiday Inn Disco on Carey Street. Tommy and Theresa dropped Mary home and continued their journey to the Holiday Inn.

As time went by, Mary gradually forgot about James. James was still in love with Mary. But he was too proud to apologize. James refused to acknowledge his own wrong.

Theresa and Tommy did all they could to make Mary forget about James. They took her out on weekends. The only thing they did not do was to find another boyfriend for Mary. Mary's grades in school improved tremendously, following the drink. Her grades climbed to the 90s by the close of the semester.

As Mary was strolling from school one afternoon, Mr. Clinton Simpson stopped his black New Yorker to offer Mary a lift. The long-windy Monrovia rain was drizzling.

Simpson said, "Hi, little girl. How far are you going?"

"I am going behind Monrovia College, on Camp Johnson Road," Mary replied.

"I can drop you there, 'cause I will pass around there. But please allow me to pass by my office for a few seconds, to collect my travelling documents."

"Thanks. I would not mind if you stop at your office to collect your papers."

Mary had not quite taken her seat in the car when Clinton Simpson started to bombard her with several and interesting questions.

"What is your name, little girl? I don't mean to underestimate you, calling you little girl. Also, I like to ask questions."

"No, I don't mind. I am Mary Tweh."

"If I know my Liberian Sociology and Geography, the name Tweh is suggestive that you are either Kru or Grebo. Are you Kru? Don't think that I am being tribalistic."

"Yes, I am Kru. Tribalism is not recognition of names per se. It is recognition of tribal identity and names, followed by favoritism. I am sure you are not giving me this lift because of my tribal or ethnic background. You are doing this out of generosity, knowing that it is raining and that I am a lady."

"That is true, Mary. This is what has affected the progress of this country over the last one hundred years. Now, one may not belong to any tribe or ethnic group and practice segregation in Liberia or throughout the world. I am speaking of class system, race, sex, nepotism, religion. Please note that I mention religion, not because I hate religion. But people use their religious preferences to segregate from other people—the Christians, the Muslims, the Hindus, the free thinkers, etc. etc. These different forms of segregation are as bad as tribalism."

"Yes, Mr. Simpson, segregation has many ramifications. Some people in Liberia tend **to** magnify tribalism only; and it is not the only form of discrimination in Liberia, or in the rest of Africa and the world at large."

"Who are your parents, Mary? You sound interesting."

"Mr. and Mrs. Tweh, the late Commissioner."

"Hon. Commissioner Tweh who died in the plane crash somewhere in Egypt?"

116

"Yes. He was my father."

"Have my sympathy."

"Thank you."

"And where is your mother?"

"She is right here in Monrovia, on Camp Johnson Read, where we live."

"Does she work?"

"No. She is too old to work."

"How many are you? Do you have brothers and sisters?"

"No, I am the only child of my mother and father; all my brothers and sisters died."

"Oh, isn't it something? How does she pay your school fees?"

"She sells bread, cookies, and coconut candies."

"Do you have any part-time job after school?"

"No. I do not work, due to many reasons."

"What are some of your reasons? Intruding into your privacy?"

"Not at all. I have applied at several offices in town, took some tests and passed with high honors. But those who are in authority or those who have the final say would not employ me. They want to go to bed with me before. And no one can induce me for a job or anything else; there is nothing wrong with falling in love with a man or boy at your working place, provided you love him; and that he is not employing you just for sex. These are some of the impediments girls are facing in Monrovia. I don't know what goes on in the other cities and parts of Liberia."

"I know just exactly what you are talking about because I have worked in many offices in town here. And I know all the dirt that we see in these offices. As a result of such immoral practices, some girls who are employed under such circumstances do not work at all. They absent themselves from work without excuse from anybody. If they go to work at all, they just sit there, talking, drinking coca-cola or eating peanuts the whole day. And mind you, they are drawing their checks out of tax payers' money."

"Exactly so, Mr. Simpson. Some people say that Monrovia girls do not want to work. But these are some of the reasons."

"What is your class now, Mary?"

"Eleventh grade."

"That's good. What is your favorite subject in school?"

"English and literature."

"What kind of literature are you studying in school?"

"English and American literature."

"Are you doing Liberian literature?"

"No. There is no authentic Liberian literature. No Liberian novels. No dramas. However, we did a few African novels, written by Nigerian, Ghanian and Kenyan authors; Liberian literature has not yet been developed.

"What a shame! What has happened to our Liberian culture or literature? Why should our students read literature which they cannot relate to their own surroundings?"

"We asked our English teacher, a Liberian, some of the same questions you are posing; and he had no good reasons to give. He did English/Literature as his major at the University of Liberia and he has been teaching for some fifteen years; and he has not written one short story. It is deplorable that some Liberians are ashamed of their own culture; most of the books written about Liberia are written by foreigners."

"We have a long way to go. But how long shall it be? After one hundred and forty-two years? ... By the way, how much do you pay for your tuition and books?"

"Fifty dollars per semester for my school fees and eighty dollars for books."

"That's too much, isn't it? I wonder how many students can afford that amount in Monrovia? I mean the masses."

"Not many students can, really. You know, CWA is one of the expensive schools in Monrovia. In fact, ninety percent of the students at CWA are children of prominent citizens in the country. If you see any students from poor families at CWA, they are either on scholarships or living with big shots in Monrovia; otherwise, no poor man can send his child to CWA. This is why my mother is struggling very hard. She's a widow and her parents are not living, either."

"I see. I think your school problem is grave."

"What to do, Mr. Simpson? We have to try our best."

Instead of passing to his office to collect his travelling papers as he said earlier, Clinton Simpson drove along United Nations Drive, by way of the American Embassy and onto Camp Johnson Road, talking with Mary. Their chat did not finish when Clinton reached Camp Johnson Road.

He ventured to kiss Mary, while at the same time placing a ten dollar bill in her breast. She resisted the kiss; but she took the ten dollars.

Simpson was a handsome man, though.

He said, "I see you again, Mary. It was nice talking with you. I wish we could sit down somewhere and talk some more, say tomorrow. But I will not be in town again for a week. I leave Monrovia this evening for Paris, France, to attend a conference of engineers. Maybe when I come back, I will contact you at CWA. And we can sit and talk things over, at my house. You can bring your friends over in the evening, for a drink. I am always there. Okay?"

119

"Nothing is wrong with that. I will be available when you return. I will tell my best friend, Theresa, and her boyfriend, Tommy. I see you."

"See you, Mary."

Mary arrived home earlier than usual in recent weeks. And the mother inquired why she got home sooner that day.

Chapter 14

"Why you came home sooner today, baby?"

"It is drizzling, Ma, and I got a lift. I had no money to pay taxi."

"Lift? Who brought you home? James?"

"No, Ma. I told you before that James and I are not on good terms, because of what he did to me. Mr. Clinton Simpson brought me."

"That old witch?"

"Oh, is he a witch? I did not know that, Ma. At least he did not impress me as a witch, I think that he is a gentleman."

"No! He is a wicked man. Don't you know that he hates women like how we hate black snake?"

"But. . . but, . but. . .Ma?"

"What you want to tell me, baby? That old witch can abuse women, 'cause he is sexually impotent."

"How do you know, Ma? Have you seen or met him before? How do you know that he is impotent?"

"I know because we don't see any woman with him, with all the money he has; and people tell us that he is impotent. You know very well that news can't hide in Monrovia. I have not seen him."

"Is that all? Suppose he does not want to walk with women or ride with women in his car? Does that mean that he is impotent? That he is a wicked man?"

"He's not like other Monrovia men, my child? Most of the men in town like women like how ants like sugar."

"But Ma, suppose he does not want to have children or he just cannot bear children?"

"Then he should not offer you any lift."

"Come on, Ma. Even if he offers me lift, or if I am in love with him? I am not saying that I am in love with him, but it could be."

"Look, my child, we African women love our men more if we bear children for them. Children are one of the important and direct benefits we get from marriage. You must have children if you get married. What will you do with an impotent man?"

"Not these days, Ma. We love these days because of love, not necessarily children. Who knows whether I will have children as you did?"

"All I know, Mary, is that you will marry the man that I want."

"Who is that man?"

"Emmanuella T. James Dennis, the boy at the College of West Africa. That's the boy I like for you. Nobody else."

"Suppose I am not in love with James now?"

"Unless I ain't born you, you don't come from my belly before you will marry any man that I don't accept; you must do what I say."

"Look, Ma, sit down and let me tell you my free mind today, especially my love affair. You are not the one to tell me whom to love or whom to marry. In the case of James, I did not know any better. It was nice however, on his part that he wrote you, requesting for your approval. But it was left with me to either accept him or reject him. I must enjoy that freedom to think for myself. I have not told you that Mr. Simpson is my boyfriend. But if I love him, we can go ahead and do our thing. You can't stop it, even though I respect you as my mother; but you have nothing to do with my love affair. It is strictly private."

"Mary, my child, you are telling a black lie, from the bottom of hell. Unless I die today or tomorrow before you will marry any boy that I don't approve of. This is how we were brought up in this country; and this is how we will train you people, the younger generation. In the first place, where does this Clinton Simpson come from? Who knows him in Monrovia and in the country? What is his future in the country?"

'Oh, Mother, you should be ashamed of yourself. You still have the mentality: Where he comes from? Who knows him? Let me ask you a question. Who knew my father, Tweh, when he married you in Monrovia? He was just another 'country Kru boy,' as you all termed him in those days. But he turned out to be one of the best students ever graduated from Liberia College, now the University of Liberia. He faithfully served this government and rose to the position of Provincial Commissioner in the then Department of Interior.

"He was not known from the beginning; but he made himself famous in this country through his academic achievements, his worth, his contributions to this society. I don't care where anybody comes from. We are all Liberians and Africans. We are all members of the family of man. I have no case against any class or race of people."

"My child, I gave birth to you; you must do what I say. I care less about what you are saying about race, class system, and what have you."

"Okay, Ma, there is no need to argue. In fact, I should not argue with you. But I have told you what I feel about my life, how I should do things on my own, and how I should make my own decisions."

"Time will tell, baby," Lu concluded.

From the onset, Mary admired Clinton Simpson; it was to her taste that Simpson extended her the invitation to visit his house. And the position which old lady Lucretia took against Simpson only made Mary love him more and more. Mary told her friends, Tommy and Theresa, about Clinton Simpson.

"Theresa," Mary said, "do you know one Clinton Simpson?"

"Yes. I know him very well. He and Tommy worked at Joe Hansen for some time before he resigned. Simpson was one of the best engineers at Joe Hansen, but he left Joe Hansen, due to some reason. Tommy should know why he left."

"Simpson left Joe Hansen because he and his immediate boss could not agree," Tommy pointed out. "Simpson knew more than the so-called boss, and the boss could not stomach Simpson. He felt that Simpson was a threat to his position; and therefore he made things so impossible for him, that he had to resign his job. And Simpson is not a proud man. He went about his business, doing his *work,* " Tommy explained.

"Why are you asking me about Simpson, Mary?" Theresa asked.

"I met him yesterday while walking from school. I think you had left already for home when he met me down the road. He offered me a lift and we talked lengthily, from Broad Street to U.N. Drive and on Camp Johnson Road, just talking from one topic to the other. He seems to be an intelligent man."

124

"Yes, Mary, he is very smart. This is why he does not talk too much with people who have nothing to contribute toward a good conversation. And people generally misconstrue him, thinking that he is too proud and selfish. It is not so. He is an intellectual," Tommy said.

"I think so, too, Tommy. He spoke at the commencement exercises of Suehn Academy from which my older sister graduated last year. He delivered a powerful address. It seems that he is a British, trained engineer; his 'Oxford English' is superb," Theresa said.

Mary observed, "It seems that he likes dressing, I mean good clothes. He matched from his toe to the head, on the day I rode with him. Simpson had on gray shoes, light gray socks, gray trousers and a light T shirt. His hair is well trimmed. A clean cut and well-dressed gentleman."

"Oh, yes! Girls used to fight for him at Jos Hansen. All the girls wanted him, for his cleanliness and his intelligence. Every woman wants a clean man. You don't see the kind of car Simpson rides in Monrovia?" Tommy asked.

"That is a tough car, Tommy... Simpson is gone to Paris for a conference of engineers, for a week, to represent his organization. He would like to see me when he gets back from Paris. He also invited some of my friends to his house upon his return. I will take you and Theresa with me, Tommy, to visit him one evening. I think I like him."

"That's good. We will go with you, Mary. I know where he lives. He is on Twelfth Street, not too far from my place. He finished his house one and a half years ago and he lives there all by himself," Tommy asserted.

"We will be there in full. I hope that my friend will find a nice boyfriend," Theresa added.

"Yes. I hope to find a good boyfriend. Seemingly, Simpson is the right one; I will not turn him down. I will prove to James that I can find a nice man, if not a better man than he."

The news of Mary's association with Simpson soon got around in school and the neighborhood. Some boys and girls at CWA had seen when Mary rode with Simpson for the first time; her friends and classmates joked her about having a "black car" in Monrovia. Even her teachers knew of the jokes.

Mary's mother told some relatives and neighbors that Mary was in love with Clinton Simpson. Mary's aunts and cousins and other relatives were bitterly against Simpson; they just did not want to hear his name, on the ground that he did not spend any time with women.

In the meantime, some students told Dennis that his girl friend was in love with Clinton Simpson; and James summoned Mary to a face-to-face confirmation of the Simpson news.

James was jealous.

"Mary, I want to see you," James told Mary during recess.

"But you can see me here," she replied.

"I can see you, but I want to talk with you."

"Say what you want to say, James."

"Let's go in the classroom."

"You can say it here; some students are still in the classroom."

"Okay, I will say it right here. Are you in love with Clinton Simpson?"

"No, I am not in love with him."

"You are lying."

"Have I lied to you before?"

"Yes. You always ride with him."

"Did you see me riding with him? If so, what's wrong with that? I did ride with him, but once. And I have not denied it to you, either. Why did you say that I have lied to you?"

"This is not a courtroom, Mary. Give me my gold finger ring, because I do not have any 'big car' in Monrovia," James said forcefully.

"James, it seems that you do not love me. Even if I were in love with Simpson, I do not think that you should have approached me like this, especially while we are in school, with all the students around. You could have come over to my house and talked this over with me, not in school. In the second place, what has happened to all your girlfriends? You should go and dance with all four of your girlfriends that you had at the dance that night. *I* don't trouble you; *I* am quiet and composed."

"I don't care for any kind of approach. Please give me my finger ring."

Mary politely took the ring from her finger and gave it to James. He walked away calmly.

James broke his own neck too soon; he saw the writing on the wall, that he was out of the world of Mary; Mary did not bother him in school. She had no time. Better days were ahead for her.

When Simpson returned from Paris, he drove to CWA at the close of a school day in order to find Mary. Mary and Theresa were walking down the steps when Simpson parked his long car near the school steps. Mary saw and recognized Simpson's car; Simpson also saw Mary, walking down the steps.

Chapter 15

"Come in, Mary. I stopped by to see whether your school was over," Simpson said, winding the glass down.

"Come in, Theresa. Let's ride with Mr. Simpson. Hello, Mr. Simpson. Meet my friend, Theresa. Theresa, Mr. Clinton Simpson," Mary introduced Theresa to Simpson while she sat down in the front seat.

"Hi, Theresa. Nice meeting you."

"It is nice meeting you, too," Theresa replied.

"When you got back?" Mary asked Simpson.

"I came last night, about 11:45 p.m."

"How was the trip to Paris?"

"I think the trip was rewarding. I met people from a hundred and fifty countries, all over the world. I think I learned a lot from the people *I* met, exchanging views on current. issues in the engineering profession. *I* am happy to have made the trip. At least I made fresh contacts with some parts of the world."

"That is nice. I told my friend, Theresa, and her boyfriend, Tommy about you. And they are willing to go with me at your house, as you said before leaving for Paris."

"Is that right?"

"Yes. Mary told us about you, how you gave her a ride from school the other day. My boyfriend, Tommy, knows you very well. He worked with Jos Hansen some time ago, at the time you were also working there," Theresa remarked.

"Oh, yes. I was with Jos Hansen for some time. I know Tommy very well, also; he is tall with light skin. Right?"

"Yes, Mr. Simpson," Theresa replied.

"Well, that is how it goes. The world is small. You don't know when you will meet your old friends and classmates after a long time. I have not met Tommy for a long time since I left Jos Hansen. Now I am meeting his girlfriend today. Tommy was nice to me at Jos Hansen."

"You were good to him also, Mr. Simpson. He told me several times about you, not in the negative, of course. I know you, also, especially from when you spoke at the commencement of Suehn Academy," Theresa said.

"Stop that! You were there, Theresa?"

"Yes. My older sister graduated from high school that time. So we had to be there; all of us admired your speech."

"This is more like a family reunion. Here you, Theresa, I did not know that I met you before in my life; however, it is nice that we meet again, this time to be real friends. I told Mary before I left for Paris that I would like to meet with her and some of her intimate friends, like you and Tommy, at my house. Tomorrow is Friday. Would it be all right if you come over to my house in the evening?"

"I think so. I will ask Tommy this evening. He will come over to my house this evening and I will inform him that you are back in Monrovia."

"Shall we keep the appointment, Mary?" Clinton asked.

"Yes. We will come. Friday evening is okay with us. No school on Saturday."

"I want to 'break the egg' before I drop you people on Camp Johnson Road, Theresa. I met Mary just the other day before I went away. As providence would have it, we talked for a long time; she impressed me greatly. You see, I like to talk about things that directly affect our society. To me it is useless and time-consuming to discuss international issues at the United Nations, OAU, OPEC, and other international organizations and ignore the problems in our own society or country.

"For example, it is foolish to down-cry Idi Amin at the United Nations if all or most of the countries are guilty of the same things Idi Amin is allegedly doing in his country. The Bible clearly talks about cleaning our own eyes before trying to clean the eyes of our neighbors.

"We have many problems in Liberia. Social problems. Educational problems, Corruption. Economic development. Equal distribution of wealth among the masses. What has happened to our Liberian culture? What is wrong with Liberian literature'? Why are there no Liberian novels? What is the image of Liberia to the outside world? How does the United States look at Liberia? How does the Soviet Union evaluate us, as a nation?

"These are the kinds of things that Mary and I discussed when we met for the first time. And if a girl of your age should be able to identify these problems in high school, then I have high regard for you. This is what impressed me most about Mary and for which I like her. I understand that the two of you are intimate friends. But I like direct contact. I think that Mary is listening to what I am saying, that I like her. When we meet tomorrow, we shall talk some more," Simpson concluded.

"Yes, that will be our topic of discussion tomorrow evening, Mr. Simpson. Here is Mary; she is not a child. She will speak for herself tomorrow at the house," Theresa said.

"I showed a liking for Mary when we met for the first time; I gave her something. I will not say what it was. She took it; but she refused one concession. I see you girls tomorrow evening. Have a nice day," Simpson said when he dropped the girls on Camp Johnson Road.

"We see you tomorrow," Mary and Theresa said.

"What was it that he gave you, Mary?" "Ten dollars."

"What did you refuse to do?"

"I refused to kiss him." "Where did he want to kiss you?"

"In the car, when I was getting down."

"Why you did not kiss him on the jaw?"

"Because I did not know him. Now I know him."

Simpson kept his word. He organized the party at his house on that Friday evening. He was not popular with his neighbors in Sinkor. Some of the people who lived near Simpson marked him as a selfish man. He hardly talked with his neighbors, because most of them had nothing to offer, in the way of discussion.

Some of the neighbors were not working. Simpson's neighbors were gossipers. They sat indoors the whole day, discussing the lives of other people, some of whom they had never even seen. A man who idles must gossip.

Simpson was the complete opposite of the people who lived near him. He had nothing to do with other people's private business. He could care less about what Jose Thomas did to his wife on Broad Street; what food Mary Koon cooked on Saturday morning in New Kru Town; or what the family next door ate for their breakfast.

131

While it is true that Simpson was concerned and aware of the conditions of the masses, he took no pleasure in meddling into the personal affairs of other people.

The neighbors watched Simpson every morning getting into his car to go to work and come back from work in the evening. They spied on him to see whether he came home from work with a woman or not. They investigated as to whether he was married or not, whether he had any relatives living with him; they wanted to know his sexual preference. Was he homosexual? To their disappointment, they saw no boys in his house or riding with him when he came back from work or anywhere else.

The neighbors were curious to know whether Simpson could sponsor lavish parties during Christmas, New Year, or Independence seasons.

His birthday was another mystery to them. When was his birthday? We do not even know the birthday of that selfish man. They tried to tail him, for personal information; but they could not get one word from Simpson.

One thing they were aware of: Simpson was a kind and considerate man. He was always willing to give any worthy financial assistance: paying the tuition of deserving students in high schools, colleges and universities; paying hospital bills for the old and needy; contributing toward social welfare organizations in the country and abroad; and paying hut taxes for poor people from the interior of Liberia. But he did not give his money to anyone who could work but did not want to work. Such generosity encourages laziness and a 'don't care' attitude.

He had only one friend, Magnus T. S. G. Tarpeh, a Kru boy who was also born in Ghana. Tarpeh and Simpson attended the same secondary school and college in Ghana, played on the same soccer team, and went to Liberia together.

He invited Tarpeh to the drink at his house.

To most of the neighbors, the evening was special. They heard loud music from Simpson's house that evening, beginning at 6:30 p.m.

Later in the evening, at 8 p.m., Simpson drove to town to collect Mary and Tarpeh. Tommy and Theresa walked from Tommy's apartment, which was not too far from where Simpson lived. Tommy invited two boys and two girls.

The visit of the boys and girls to Simpson's house gave rise to greater suspicion, especially when the neighbors saw Mary Tweh get out of Simpson's car.

"What is going on this evening? Is Simpson getting married? If he is getting married, to whom? Were they loving? How long were they loving? These were some of the questions Simpson's neighbors gurgled among themselves.

But the Simpson party was held on schedule. He had all kinds of Liberian dishes—rice, fafu and soup, palm butter, baked and fried chicken, okra sauce, etc. No formal speeches were made at the party.

"Have fun and enjoy yourselves, Ladies and Gentlemen." That was all Simpson said.

Two-to-two movement was the order of the evening. If a boy and girl were not eating or sitting very close together in the corner talking heart-to-heart they danced on the floor.

Mary landed in the hands of Simpson. The enjoyment was too much for Mary. She was beaming with smiles while eating, drinking, or dancing. Mary was indeed happy that someone had come into her life again.

However, she expressed fear to Simpson that she did not want another disappointment in her life. She did not hide her feelings; she told Simpson the story of James. She was very frank.

Simpson made no big promises to Mary. He said that it was up to her to make her own judgment. He avoided blowing his own horn.

The party came to an end to the satisfaction of everyone. Everybody danced, ate, and kissed very well. What else can you enjoy at a party, especially if the number of girls and boys is equal?

Mary and Simpson started going out steadily. She paid no attention to what the people were saying about her relations with Simpson. Her business was going on correctly.

Almost six months passed and Simpson proved his name and image worthy of Mary's choice. At the beginning of Mary's high school senior year, Simpson paid her school fees and bought her books and uniforms.

Simpson did not want to play any hide-and-seek game. He told Mary's mother and relatives about their love affair. But the mother did not want to see even the ground that Simpson walked on. Lu did not like Simpson.

Simpson went over to Mary's house one Saturday morning for a serious talk. Old lady Lucretia had gone to Kakata to visit her sister and the rubber farm. Mary welcomed Simpson, and he settled down in the armchair. Simpson started a quick and interesting conversation.

"Mary, dear, I came to see you and your mother, even though I know that she would not approve of what I have to say. I know that she does not like me. But for the sake of respect, I have got to tell her. I don't know what you will have to say."

"What is that, Simpson?"

"But where is your mother first? I want to meet the two of you, because it concerns her as well."

"She is gone to Kakata to see the rubber farm and her sister. The sister sent a message yesterday that the farm is

134

going bad. The undergrowth is getting higher and higher. All the workers have left the farm. My mother left this morning and may be back late this evening; I am not quite sure when."

"Shall I go home then and come back this evening or tomorrow evening?"

"No. You can tell me; I will inform her when she comes."

"Well, I came to propose engagement because as you know, I love you dearly. Can you remember and imagine that I loved you and wanted to marry you, even the very first day we met? But I have been very hesitant to come here and tell your mother because I know she does not want to see me. There are many reasons why I would like to marry you, although I cannot give you gold, silver, or diamonds.

"Most of the people at my working place, especially girls, are against our relations. My neighbors, too, are very bitter about it. Even my immediate chief knows of our going out; the people in Monrovia told him; I know it is private but I don't know why they have to probe into my personal affair. I don't trouble anybody in town or at my working place. I don't have any girlfriend at my working place. But I don't understand."

"I know what you mean, Simpson. It is good that you did not meet my mother here. She does not approve of the lifts you usually give me, the tuition you paid for me, or the monthly allowance you provide. She'd hate it all the more if we were engaged in her presence. She has rallied all our relatives to come and talk to me. My grandfather in New Kru Town, old man Wesseh and Grandmother were here last night to talk to me. Of course, they have no case against you.

"You know, several times you and I went to New Kru Town to see them. They like you a lot. But my mother and her relatives are opposed to you. I don't know what you did to them. But I love you too; and I think we can get married if you can withstand the forces of my relatives, especially my mother.

"I know it would not be easy for us; but if we love one another, we can send the rest of the world to hell. I would advise you therefore, that you address a letter to her, and I will give it to her when she returns from Kakata this evening."

"My only question is, why should all the people whom I know be against me? Why should they tail me all the time? What have I done to them? They don't even know me very well."

"Don't you know, Simpson, that the eye of society is powerful; that it focuses on you and me, whether we like it or not? We are slaves of society, especially in towns and villages where everybody knows everybody. It is not easy to keep an eye on people in large cities, like New York, Chicago, Paris, or London. People in big cities are always busy, working. No one has any time for the next person. Even people with whom you live in the same building may never see you in big cities. Yet, even with the astronomical population in big cities, the 'eye of the law' is watching everyone.

Where did you get that large sum of money to buy big car or house? How long have you been working at a job before you can afford to buy a car? If you are not working at all, where did you get money from? Are you on welfare? Are you a dope pusher? Are you a pimp? The law and law enforcing agencies keep probing these questions. To some degree, the eye of society is meddling into our personal affairs. How long shall people continue to gossip? As long as man exists. Don't mind the 'noise of the market' or else you will not buy anything from the market. Go right ahead and write the letter to mother."

"Okay, I will write the letter. Please give me a piece of paper and an envelope. I can write the letter right here."

136

"No problem. Here are the paper and envelope. Use all the persuasive language you know. I don't know whether engineers are persuasive like lawyers and diplomats."

"We shall try our engineering diplomacy."

Simpson prepared the letter. It was well written; but the fact that his name was attached to the bottom of the letter was all that mattered to Lucretia.

He had a long and impressive chat with Mary. Mary told him to leave earlier than he had planned. Simpson yielded to Mary's advice and left by midday.

Mary gave her mother the letter as soon as she returned from Kakata. She told Mary, "My child, you will be the cause for my old and protracted sickness to come back and kill me, even now. I know that I will soon leave this world, just for worries, 'cause I don't like that man."

"Mother, please be frank with me, as your daughter, and tell me why you don't like Mr. Simpson."

"I don't like him because he cannot bear children, baby girl; and as such I will never permit him to marry you. All the people in our neighborhood tell me that they have not one day seen a woman with Simpson. He may be a gentleman, yes. He helped us to pay your school fees, yes. He gives you some money at the end of every month, yes. But material things without children are worthless. We want children!"

"Mother, that is your belief, not mine. Children are not the only results we reap from marriage. We get love, tender care, and affection from the one whom we love, not children only. How sure are you, Ma, that I will have children? And have you not seen a man and a woman divorced, even though they have children? Children alone cannot solve their problems. I do agree with you that children are nice to have in a family. But that is not all there is. I know a couple just opposite our house who were married for fifteen years and had seven children. They were divorced just the other day. They had bad problems with all the children."

"All our family people have children; not one of us is without children. And for that matter, you, too, will have children."

"That is not a good yardstick, Mother. That you had children does not mean that I will also have children. What has happened to Solomon D. Kotella? His mother and father had about twenty-five children. Since Solomon got married when I was about ten years old, he and his wife have not had any children; and they are living together happily. Children are nature's gift; you can't force them, or else the millionaires or the money people we have in Monrovia would have bought all the children they need from God or nature. But you cannot buy them."

"You children of these days have no respect for older people, especially your parents, your belly-born mothers. Not when I am living! I don't see my way clear seeing you with Clinton Simpson as your husband. Hell no!"

The dialogue grew tense, especially when Mary stood for what she believed and what any young person would believe and act on.

Mary told Simpson the outcome of the letter. But he paid Mary regular visits, even when the mother was there at home. He never showed disrespect for her. Simpson was always polite, not only to old lady Lucretia, but to all the people he had contact with.

Chapter 16

It is by far better for a girl to make a unilateral decision and select her boyfriend (husband to be) than for the selection to be influenced by some outside force. The same is true in the case of a boy courting a girl for his wife.

This is not to suggest that parents or guardians should not 'make some tangible suggestions to their children regarding marriage. But authoritative suggestions, such as, you must marry this girl or you have to marry that boy or you must marry within your own social status are foolish.

The reasons are simple and clear. Husband and wife should live together as one body. In order for their marriage to last, the husband and wife must study the likes, dislikes, and attitudes of each other over a protracted period of time. It must be agreed upon that the opinions and suggestions of the wife are as important as the husband's. They must be a team.

In order for the wife and husband to live together happily, they must share some things in common. Where are they coming from? What are their ambitions in life? What do they want most, out of their union? Wealth? Children? Happiness? Are they married because of their sexual preference? Are they married because of their religion? Do they have a similar level of education?

In other words, the wife and husband must have a "meeting of the minds" in their lifetime contract or else their union will collapse. If the marriage is erected on shaky ground, it will crumble and fall flat.

Oftentimes we attend weddings, Western-style weddings—and we pay keen attention to some of the hackneyed questions posed by the officiating priest or justice of the peace. Often, when the priest asks the question, "Will you keep this woman as your wedded wife and forsake all others until death?" there is sarcastic laughter following the question. Yet, in all the marriage ceremonies I have attended, the wife and husband have answered this question in the affirmative.

Why then should the audience burst into laughter? They laugh because they know that the man and woman are not telling the truth, even before God. They laugh because some of the people in the audience, even the so-called religious fanatics, are not keeping their marital vows.

What a mockery of God! What a mockery of the Christian church!

Why should men subject themselves to conditions which they cannot keep? Why should we make public declarations before men and God, knowing that we will not keep the promises that we make?

Mary Tweh made up her mind to marry Clinton Simpson. Her decision was not influenced by anybody. She was in love with Simpson, perhaps for several reasons. Mary was committed to her conscience.

Old lady Lucretia could not rest her mind, regarding the relations between Simpson and Mary. She went to New Kru Town to complain to Mary's grandfather, old man Wesseh.

Lu told the old man that it was his responsibility, as a man, to change Mary's mind. She concluded that perhaps Mary refused to listen to her because of her sex, and she being an old lady, at that.

Old man Wesseh expressed indignation at the pig-headed behavior of Mary. He assured Lucretia that he would get in contact with Mary as soon as possible and that Mary would listen to his advice.

Old lady Lu left New Kru Town in high spirits. She was happy because old man Wesseh was going to take stern action against Mary and Simpson.

Lucretia had the story all wrong. Old man Wesseh did not tell Lu the truth concerning the relations of Mary and Simpson. Several times, Simpson and Mary went to New Kru Town to visit the old man and his wife. Simpson had made his intention known to the old man and his wife, and they had accepted Simpson with open arms.

The old man invited Simpson and Mary to New Kru Town one evening. He wanted to hear, for the second time, Simpson's intentions toward Mary.

Simpson and Mary drove to New Kru Town to honor the invitation of the old man. Simpson carried with him a case of club beer, two bottles of gin, and two bottles of whisky, as well as one big club bottle of cane juice.

Wesseh and his wife were already waiting when Simpson and Mary arrived. The old man and his whole house extended a red carpet reception for Mary and Simpson.

Without any formal ceremonies, Simpson took the drinks from the trunk of the car and gave them to the old man and his wife. They were so happy for the drinks.

Wesseh said, "The drinks are too expensive; you could have only bought cane juice instead. We don't drink this kind of expensive liquor around here. We drink our homemade cane juice, and we like it. For one thing, it is stronger and by far cheaper than gin or whisky. However, we are thankful to you and Mary."

'Well, old man, sometimes we need a change in what we eat, drink, or wear. I am sure you ate palm butter yesterday. Today, maybe your wife prepared soup or dry rice with smoked fish, just for a change in your diet. This is why we bought the gin, whisky, and beer. You can see that we did not forget your favorite drink, cane juice."

"Thank you very much. Have your seats and let's talk as father and children. Old lady Lu was here the other day to complain about you and Mary. She is totally opposed to you, on the grounds that you are from nowhere and that no one in Monrovia knows you, even though you maintain a good job. When Lu told me this, I laughed in my heart, because I know the hell we caught when Tweh, Mary's father, married Lu some twenty years ago. Lu's father, the late Hon. Mantarda, told us in plain English that Tweh was a 'country Kru boy,' that Tweh was not known in Monrovia and therefore could not marry his daughter, Lucretia. Mantarda wanted his daughter to marry someone from Monrovia, Harper City, Buchanan, or Greenville.

"The only reason why Tweh was allowed to marry Lu was because she was pregnant while they were attending Liberia College. Lu and Tweh were classmates, and the Mantarda family did not want any scandal in the family.

"Today, the story is almost the same. The same Lu who was married to a man who was a Kru man and was not known in Monrovia, is saying that Mary should not marry you because you are not known. I am only presenting the facts as they were some twenty years ago so that the two of you will know. My wife knows what I am saying. This is our family history - we will never forget it.

142

"I am quite sure, Simpson, that you may have heard of my son, Commissioner Tweh, and his achievements in life before his untimely death in a plane crash in Egypt. He was a Kru man, but that made no difference. He taught mathematics at Liberia College. He travelled extensively in the interior of Liberia, administering government policies. Tweh worked for the Department of Interior, now the Ministry of Local Government, Urban Reconstruction and Development in various capacities. His last mission was to represent the Government of Liberia to the international conference in Cairo, Egypt, when he met his death. He died in service! What else can a man do before he will be known or patriotic to his country?

"Definitely, Lucretia was and is still proud of Tweh. Lu's father had high regards for Commissioner Tweh after their marriage. The president of this country had confidence in my son. In fact, it was the president who designated him to represent this government at the Cairo conference because the Secretary of Interior was out of the country on sick leave. Was he not a famous man?"

Simpson responded, "I did not know all of these facts, old man. But these are the kind of problems we have had and are still facing in Liberia. I feel that in order to develop this country, Liberians should think and act as a people and not divided people. I feel that people who were born in Monrovia or other cities in the country should be willing to live say, in Tchien, Zorzor, or Gbarnga, in order to develop those parts of the country. I think that our human resources and development efforts should permeate all the sectors of the country. And the only way through which we will achieve these goals is to go into the rural areas, live with the masses of the people, be a part of them, and help educate them.

143

"It is a shame that some of the boys and girls who were born in the interior and went to school in Monrovia do not want to go back to their homes. They prefer living in Monrovia and other urban areas to living in their own homes. This is not different from superiority or discrimination against our own people. In this particular case, I would not force Mary to be with me. I know that she loves me, and I love her also. I think that it is okay. And I think that if anybody tries to break our relations, that person will fail."

"You see, Grandpa," Mary said, "I have told mother repeatedly that the mentality of yesterday cannot hold today. Things are changing very, very fast in Liberia. Things will change even faster in the years ahead than we can imagine. You made reference to my father. I have also told Ma the same thing, because she long ago had told me everything about what happened before she and my father were married.

"Simpson and I met some time ago and I love him. He loves me too. Most importantly, he cares for my well-being. I am not saying this because Simpson is right here with us. You can't just say you love a girl or woman and not know how she eats. Simpson pays my school fees, buys my books and gives me a monthly allowance, knowing that mother and I are not working.

He buys our monthly provisions—rice, oil, soap and everything that we need for the whole month. He just appropriated some money to develop the rubber farm that mother could not maintain, due to lack of funds. It is not the matter of the money he is spending, but the willingness to do so. How many men in Monrovia, Grandpa, could assist a girl like me? Of course, not many men. I mean, a limited few. Simpson and I think alike; we sit and talk things over like equals. He respects my thinking and I do the same to him. This is compatibility, which most are lacking. To be realistic,

Grandpa, I think that we will make it. I have decided to marry Simpson."

"One advice which I will give you, Simpson, is, as a man, you must be able to play a major role in whatever the two of you have decided to do. You have to protect her interest all of the time; I mean if she is not in the wrong. Be fatherly to Mary. Control your temper because women are firing sometimes, without meaning any harm. I know that it would be very difficult for you to. get married. Old lady Lu will do everything to discourage you and Mary. But you should do as your conscience will lead you. That is my fatherly advice."

"We are grateful to you, old man Wesseh. I will try my best to make Mary happy," Simpson concluded.

Mrs. Wesseh had earlier prepared a big bowl of *fufu* and soup, with fresh fish, pig feet and half-dry meat and okra. Simpson and Mary never expected any food from old lady Wesseh.

The food was delicious. Simpson and Mary felt as heavy as lead when they swallowed the big bowl of *fufu*. Simpson could hardly drive when they were going back to Sinkor.

"Shall we pass by Theresa's?" Mary asked.

"Sure. Why not? Let's stop by her house so you can tell her what old man Wesseh explained about the old lady."

"Yes. This is one of the reasons I want us to see Theresa before reaching home. Theresa and I share our experiences with one another. This is why we are so intimate. People do not understand why we are so friendly."

"I know that Theresa is a genuine friend to you, Mary; you don't have to tell me. I have seen it."

Theresa jumped outside to greet Mary and Simpson when Simpson parked his car in the yard. She was home playing and recording African music.

Theresa said, "Come right in and have a seat. What can I offer you to drink?"

"Anything," Simpson replied.

"I am sipping on Mateus wine. I also bought some fresh palm wine at the General Market this morning; it is in the refrigerator. You want the palm wine or the Mateus wine?"

"I think we will try the palm wine," Mary suggested. Theresa brought out a gallon of palm wine and set it on the table. It was icy cold and strong.

"Help yourselves. What is happening this evening? Where are you coming from?" Theresa asked.

"We are coming from New Kru Town to see my grandfather. Ma has done it again. She carried my complaint to grandfather, concerning Simpson and me."

"Is that true?"

"Yes. The old man invited us to hear our side of the story," Simpson said.

"What was the complaint?"

"She went to old man Wesseh so he will change my mind from Simpson. Ma does not want to see Simpson with me; also, she said that if Simpson and I are married, she will disown me."

"That is a serious situation, Mary. And what did old man Wesseh say?"

"He cannot say anything to the contrary. He only advised us, especially Simpson, on what he should do as a man."

"What are your plans toward Mary, Simpson?"

"I plan to marry her as soon as she is graduated from high school. And that is not too far again. I think that you all graduate in two months. Right?"

"Yes. Our graduation is in December. My boyfriend, Tommy, is also graduating in December."

"What is Tommy planning to do after his high school graduation?" asked Mary.

"He might get a scholarship to go away for a bachelor's degree in Economics. That will take about four years."

"During the four years, what will happen to him? How will you manage, too?"

"That is the question, Mary. Tommy and I have been together for some three to four years. We decided that after our high school graduation, we should get married, work and go on to college at the University of Liberia. But he would like to go away because some Liberians do not respect our own education.

"If a fellow, for example, did B.S. degree in Economics at the University of Liberia or Cuttington College and is employed, he would earn less than a guy with the same academic degree from either the United States or England. We think that our own educational system is inferior. This is why Tommy wants to go abroad.

"On one level, he is correct. This is what they do here in Liberia, I mean employers. I have tried to tell Tommy not to go; but he would not listen to me. I try to convince him for his own protection and mine. Who knows what will happen to him when he goes to the States? American women are rough, when it comes to chasing men. Of course, I would not sit here and wait for him for four years, for I know he would not wait for me. We are in flesh."

"I think that your problem is grave also, Theresa. Try and solve it the best way you can. Sit and talk with Tommy to see what you can come up with. As for Simpson and me, we have decided on what to do—get married and live our lives. I may go to college later, or I may not even go."

"Yes, Mary. You and Simpson have done the right thing. You, especially, have done the right thing, to have chosen your husband before high school graduation. Stick to Simpson; and he should do the same thing also because his shame will be your shame; his disgrace is yours; his poverty your poverty; his riches your riches. Plan your lives and live as a happy, married couple."

"Yes, Theresa. Simpson is my man. This is no lip-service talk," Mary said.

Chapter 17

Lucretia Tweh began to worry about the fate of Mary, following her high school graduation. Lu had no money for Mary to continue her education at the University of Liberia or at Cuttington University College.

Lu knew, however, that Clinton Simpson could appropriate any amount of money for Mary's education, either in the country or abroad. But she would rather die and come back before she would ask Simpson for any financial assistance.

The old lady was desperate, regarding Mary's movement, especially in the night. Lu wanted to restrict Mary from going out to dances, movies, and house parties. But it was too late to bring back the hand of the clock. If Mary could go to parties and dances while she was still in high school, then it was pointless preventing her from going out after she left high school.

Old lady Lu called Mary to her room to give her some advice.

She said, "Mary, you have done tremendously well to have completed high school at this young age. I am very happy and proud of you; I wish you were a boy. As you know, I am willing to support you through college, but I do not have the means. It would have been no problem if the rubber farm in Kakata was producing rubber. I understand that authorities at the University of Liberia have raised the tuition to over one hundred percent of what students used to pay in previous years. I am sure the tuition at Cuttington College is higher, Cuttington being a mission school.

"In this connection, I would prefer it if you were to get married now so that in the next nine months or so, I will see my grandchild before I die. Who knows when I will die? I am getting old now, Mary. Definitely, I will not live another fifteen years, due to worries, hard times, and old age, and the question of your marriage is a burden to me. I keep praying over it every day. I don't know for sure what has happened to James. I need not mention the name of Simpson, because so far as I am concerned, he does not exist. He will get married to you over my dead body, in the casket, not when my two eyes are still bright and open. What you could do is to take a test and attend the Nursing School at J. F. Kennedy Hospital or enroll at one of the commercial schools in Monrovia. You could get a job faster if you are a competent secretary or a registered nurse. This is what I have to say. What suggestions do you have?"

"Thank you very much, Mother. I am grateful to you. You have done well for me for the support you have given me from the time Pa died through high school, especially in Monrovia. I do know that if you had the money to educate me through college, you would have done it without grumbling. However, not all of us will go on to college. Regarding your suggestion about nursing school, I am not interested in nursing education. To pursue any profession, Ma, you must consider many factors. Supply and demand. By that I mean that there are more nurses in Liberia these days than hospitals or clinics. The nursing profession does not pay in Liberia; the same is true in developing countries and throughout the world. If I should study nursing, when will I ever earn say, three hundred dollars per month? Unless I work for a company like LAMCO in Yekepa or Buchanan, I will never earn a good salary as a nurse.

"But I could brush up my typing and shorthand at the Commercial School on Center and Carey Streets. The school is good because I know some graduates from there, some of whom are working as executive secretaries, both in private and public sectors. Since I did typing and shorthand at CWA, the school would not be any problem to me. I need to improve my speed both in typing and shorthand, though....

"The only point that I do not agree with you on is the question of marriage. I told you many, many times that James and I are not together any more. He is not a boyfriend to me anymore. Do you know how long it has been since you saw James? I am sure he did not come to see or speak to you during our graduation, even though you presented him a gift. I think he has not come here during the last nine months. Why talk about James? You can't force a man on me, Mother. I don't think it is right on your part."

"I talk about James because that is the boy I want you to marry; I like him a lot for my son-in-law. I don't care what you say about him; he will be your man, so long I am living. If I could see him, I would talk with him so he will come around. He is still my son."

"Talk with him for what?"

"To find out from him what he is waiting for to get married to you, now that the two of you are out of high school. After all, I am the mother. If I say that James will marry you, that's it."

"Not to me, Ma. I will marry the man that I want. I have told you this before; it is nothing that I have hidden from you. I will marry Clinton Simpson."

"Mary, you will kill me if you tell me that you will marry Clinton Simpson. I just don't like the man. I cannot stand him, not even his shadow."

"Well, I can stand him because I love him. I am mature enough to know right from wrong and judge for myself. The days when parents and guardians influenced their children about engagement and marriage are over. These are modern days, when young people must be left alone to select their own wives and husbands."

"We will see whether you will marry Simpson or not. Maybe you will get married in heaven, not on earth."

"No fuss, Ma."

"In fact, Mary, you will limit your going out with Simpson this time, or else you will not live here. I am the only rooster to crow here, no one else."

"Ma, you are making a mistake. Suppose I go out of here, do you know where I will live? I am a girl and you are putting me out. I could go out and live with Simpson, which I don't want to do until we are married. I will continue to be here and I will still go out with Simpson. You can't deny me of my right to love whomsoever I want to love. I will continue to stay here until I get married. If you insist however, that I go out, fine. But you should be in the position to explain the cause for my going out to our relatives and the people in the neighborhood."

"Okay, you can stay here. But you will not go out with Simpson."

The beginning of the mother-daughter conversation was okay. But the end of their talk was fussy; they could not agree on a point—marriage.

The pressure from old lady Lu was getting greater and greater. Mary explained to Simpson that her mother threatened to put her out of the house any time.

Simpson had to act quickly. He made arrangements with the Justice of the Peace, John Sannatahum Smith, to perform the wedding ceremonies. Justice Smith agreed.

Mary's immediate family members and mother were not at the wedding. It was attended by Tommy, Theresa and Magnus Tarpeh, Simpson's friend.

But the wedding was grand, indeed, for Mary had a man to live with and Simpson a life-partner to be with; that was the most important thing.

Mary did not sleep at home that day; the next morning she went home to tell her mother that she and Simpson were married. It was hard to break the news to the old lady. Lucretia collapsed and fainted when she heard that Mary and Simpson had been married by the Justice of the Peace the previous night.

"Mary will kill me, my people. She will be the cause for my sudden death," the old lady cried when she came to herself.

All the neighbors came to hear and share the news. Mary Tweh is married! To whom? Clinton Simpson. Her new name is Mary Tweh-Simpson!

Lucretia could not do anything. It was a matter of Lucretia versus the law. Of course, the law is higher than everybody, even the lawmakers. The law is supreme.

The old lady cried as Mary packed her belongings to move to Sinkor where Simpson was living. The neighbors tried to comfort old lady Lucretia, to tell her not to cry; it was too late to do anything.

Every home has got its own problems, problems that should be solved amicably by both the wife and husband. Not every problem should be discussed with outsiders, not even the mother-in-law or father-in-law.

Mary had more than a problem in her home.

The conflict faced Mary on the very first night of her marriage. What a blow! What a shock!

Simpson had two big beds in his master bedroom. He told Mary to sleep on one of the beds. That was the worst and most shocking news Mary had ever heard in her whole life.

Was she to explore? No. It was too early to fuss. Was she to lodge complaint to her mother? No. It was too shameful and embarrassing to do so. Was she to tell Tommy and Theresa of the situation in the bedroom? No. Not all news can we tell our friends. Bedroom news should remain in the bedroom. That is how it has been; that is how it should be.

The first night Mary spent with Simpson was not different from the nights she spent with her mother, as a single girl. The first night grew tedious, gloomy, and protracted. She was miserable, almost to the point of insanity.

Mary badly needed warmth. Her home, though modern, was not far from a prison yard. The mother and relatives did not visit Mary. The neighbors cared less about Mary.

In the evening, Simpson and Mary would read local and foreign newspapers and magazines, including Time, Newsweek, Jet, and Ebony; they watched TV and listened to Radio Stations ELWA and ELBC for the newscasts. The latest they stayed up was 11 p.m., if they missed the 9 p.m. news.

Mary could not understand the attitude of her husband; she asked him to tell her what was wrong with him, or else she would divorce him. The issue was getting out of hand.

Mary and Simpson had been married for almost eleven months and they had not yet slept in one bed.

This is how she tackled the issue: "Mr. Simpson, please know that I did not marry you because of your money or property; please note also that I have been ostracized by my family, even my mother, because of you. You know that my mother, who was supposed to have given me away in marriage, was not even at my wedding, simply because I chose to be with you. But since we got married, you have not given me the comfort I need and I deserve. I need attention. I need comfort. I need superb loving. You know that I love you. Tell me what is wrong with you."

"Yes, Mary, you are correct for asking me the question. I know that you love me. If you had no love for me, you would have gone long ago, following our marriage. You are a sincere wife to me. But I am ashamed to tell you what is wrong with me. I will tell you tomorrow."

"Look, Simpson, you need not be ashamed in front of me, because I should be the closest person to you. If you cannot tell me your complaint, then I don't know in whom you will confide any secret matter. Please tell me the cause."

"I know that you are the only person I should tell all my troubles. I am aware that if I do not tell you the whole story, I would make things worse for myself. Let me tell you what happened to me in Ghana. My parents left from Kru Coast Territory, 'Liberia, and settled in the Gold Coast, now Ghana. So I was born in Ghana. But my parents, I mean my mother and father, as well as all their other five children, died in a motor accident when I was about four years of age. I was not involved in the accident because they did not carry me with them. God wanted to save one person from the whole family, and I was the only one.

"One man, Kwesi S. B. N. Kofi, and his wife, Afua, took me in as their own son. They are the only parents I know. They tried their best to educate me; but they could not adequately support me through secondary school and college, even though they were willing to do so. I had to work while attending secondary school and college. I would stop for one academic year, work and go back to school during the following year. Students are not allowed to work in Ghana.

"I was working with a blasting group in the Gold Coast Gold Mines. While working one Friday afternoon, the dynamite went off by mistake and I was castrated. I stayed in the hospital for almost nine months; the doctors gave me up. It was God who brought me back to life. I decided to return to Liberia since, in fact, no one knows of my condition in this country. Kwesi and his wife died two years ago. Unfortunately also, I have not found one relative of my parents in Liberia since I returned to this country over four years ago. And you are the only person I consider as my mother, father, brothers, and sisters."

Tears streamed from the eyes of Simpson. He burst out crying while telling the story to Mary. Mary also cried bitterly.

Chapter 18

He said, "If you divorce me, Mary, I would rather die than to live in this world. To live where again? To go back to Ghana? Here I am. I have no relatives in the whole world. They may be living somewhere in Liberia, but I don't know them. I had no one to talk to when I came home from work, until I met you. I could not befriend any girl or woman, for fear that she would spoil my name in town. Girls these days don't hide anything that happens in the bedroom. Only you and my private doctor know what happened to me in Ghana."

"I did not marry you for money, children, or material things. I did marry you because I love you. Your condition is deplorable, but I will be the last person to talk about divorce. I will never divorce you, Mr. Simpson. All you had to do was to tell me from the beginning."

Simpson jumped from his bed to kiss Mary; he asked her to repeat what she said. Simpson could not believe his ears. He was overwhelmed with joy.

"I told you, Mr. Simpson, that I will not divorce you. You are mine forever, no matter what the circumstances may be."

"Thank you very much, Mary. I do not know how to categorize you, for your strong nature. What you have done for me is more than dying for me. This is more than sacrifice. I want to suggest something to you."

"What is that?"

"You can have a boyfriend, Mary. We are in flesh. I know what it means for you to deny yourself sex, just for me. I know what it means to be sexually stranded. Even with my condition, I do have a terrific sexual drive. But the boyfriend should not know of my condition. I don't even want to know him."

"No, Mr. Simpson. No way. I cannot do it, so long as I am married to you. One of the alternatives would be to see our private doctor. We can give him say, between two and five hundred dollars so he will tell my mother that I am pregnant; mother would then spread the news of my pregnancy like a wild fire."

"Really? You think that Dr. Simatar Cooper will agree to tell your mother that you are pregnant?"

"Why not? Don't you know that money can make the devil laugh? You can use money to maneuver the thinking of people. Why do you think politicians use money to run their campaigns? We will not give Dr. Cooper any check. We will give him raw cash, and you know that he will not refuse the money. What is more, he knows my mother very well. They have been friends for years. And she would readily believe the doctor. You know very well that he is one of the best gynecologists in Monrovia, if not in the whole country. Who will not believe a gynecologist when he declares any woman or girl pregnant?"

"That is true, Mary. Even law courts would believe anything the doctor says. I think we should give him three hundred dollars. Look under the novel with the black cover. We should have under the book about six hundred dollars; take out three hundred dollars for the doctor and place the money in the envelope. I will call the doctor as if I am sick; and he will be here in a minute."

"Okay, call the doctor to see whether he is there or not. Doctors are always on their feet, attending their patients."

Simpson rang up Dr. Cooper and asked him to come over to his place right away. As the private doctor of the Simpsons, the doctor hurriedly dressed and drove to their house.

"Hello, Mr. and Mrs. Simpson," the doctor greeted them. "What is the matter? Who is sick?"

"Have a seat, Dr. Cooper. No one is sick here. But Mr. Simpson called you for an important matter. I am sure that you know the condition of Mr. Simpson—I mean his terrible accident in Ghana. You know, Doctor, as Liberians and Africans, everybody in Monrovia, especially my mother, would like to see me pregnant, since we got married more than ten months ago. As a responsible, married woman, I cannot discuss this with anybody, not even my mother, besides you, our private doctor. This is a problem for our family.

"We would like you to dispel the rumors that my husband is sexually impotent, by telling my mother that I am pregnant. We know that you can do it; we know that you will do it for us, to save our faces from shame. We have confidence in you, Dr. Cooper. Every profession has got its own secrets. You doctors talk about 'privileged information' between the doctor and his patient. This is one of the times we would really want you to help us; we would like to keep this a top secret among the three of us."

"Mr. Simpson, you listened to what your wife has just said? Are you in agreement with what she said?"

"Yes, Dr. Cooper. This is why we have called you here. Her mother is very disturbed about Mary not getting pregnant. In fact, she does not visit us at all. She has not even come here one day since we got married, simply because the daughter is not pregnant"

"We know, Doctor, that we cannot pay you for this kind of service to us. However, we thought to give you a little purse of $300, not paying you at all," Mary said.

"Is it a check?"

"No, Doctor, it is in cash. Here is it in this envelope."

"Okay, Mary. I will meet with your mother and I will report back to you the result of my talk with her. I know that these confidential matters do come up between doctors and their patients. Leave the rest with me. I will know how to frame the story to old lady Lucretia tomorrow. Everything will be taken care of."

"Thank you very much, Dr. Cooper. Simpson and I are so happy that you came to help us. We could not have gotten this kind of assistance from anybody other than a responsible person like you. We are depending on you."

"Okay then, take it easy. I see you all tomorrow. Take me for what I said. Everything will be all right by tomorrow."

"Bye now, Doctor," Simpson and Mary said.

Dr. Cooper drove by old lady Lucretia's house on Camp Johnson Road the next day, as he promised.

"Hello, Ma Lu. How are you today?"

"Who is that?" Lu asked while coming from the kitchen.

"Dr. Simatar Cooper."

"Dr. Cooper, my son, what wind blew you around here this morning? Long time no see. Have seat, Doctor."

"Thank you. I came to supervise the vaccination team at Monrovia College. You know we are vaccinating all the students within the Monrovia Consolidated School System against cholera. There are a few cases of cholera in some West African countries and we have to take due precaution."

160

"Tell me this, my child. You say what? Cholera? That is a terrible sickness."

"That is true, Ma Lu. But there is no need to panic. Cholera is always on a rampage in dirty places, slum areas like West Point, Buzi Quarters or Clara Town. I think this year we have had only three cases of cholera from West Point. We also treated a few patients near our border with Guinea. Other than that, there's no need to worry, Ma Lu.... How are Mary and her husband, Mr. Simpson?"

"My child, don't ask me about those people. Since they got married I have not seen them. They had a secret wedding, you know. And that is hurting me so bad. I will never forget or forgive that old witch, Simpson, who stole my daughter and married her. Even though Simpson tries to reach me. But no way. He has on several occasions come here to see me, but I don't want to even talk with him!"

"Why, Ma Lu? You are the only parent I know of, who should take care of Mary. Why can't you forgive her? I know several young people who got married without telling their parents. But after some time, the parents forgave them. We cannot control the thinking of our children these days, Ma Lu. Reconsider your stand and visit them one day."

"From the beginning of Simpson's relations with Mary, I opposed him bitterly, even now. We heard, my child, that that gentleman, Simpson, is impotent. People in Monrovia told us. You know Monrovia people cannot cover their mouths. They may talk plenty, but some of their talk is true. And I think that they told the truth, for Mary and Simpson have been married for over eight months and she is not pregnant as yet. Now, what kind of man is he? For nothing man?"

"Who told you, Ma Lu? Let me see, Mary Simpson was in my clinic about two weeks ago and she is pregnant. Simpson is not impotent."

"Stop that, Doctor! My God! The people in this town can lie too much! I will go and see my daughter and her husband tomorrow. My people, come and hear my story! Mary Tweh-Simpson is pregnant! I cannot believe my ears, Dr. Cooper."

"It is true, Ma Lu. Don't believe what these people say around town about other people. Sometimes they say things they have no proof of. I have no cause to lie."

"Oh no, Dr. Cooper. I would be the last person to say that you lie. You are a professional man. That is your profession. I don't doubt you a bit."

"The only thing I have to say is that she needs to go abroad for medication. It seems that Mary has a weak back and low blood. If her back is not checked immediately, especially during her pregnancy, she might have an abortion."

"Is that so?"

"Yes. But we have sent people abroad several times with the same trouble. She will be okay if she takes the right treatment. That means, she will not work and sit up for a long time or stand up on her feet for a long time. I am happy that Simpson does not even allow her to work. She does not even cook. They have a cook at home."

"Well, thank God, Dr. Cooper. I hope that you will try for my daughter. That is the only child I have. And I have been praying for a child for my daughter, long even before she got married to Simpson. I hope that she will bear the child safely. God will be with her."

"I will do my best, Ma Lu. She will have the baby without any trouble, the sooner she goes abroad, either to West Germany or the United States, for medical care."

"Thank you very much, Dr. Cooper. I see you again."

"Yes. I will see you again. We will work here at the school for about two weeks; I will try to get some tablets for you and bring them over in one week. Your hands look pale to me. Maybe you need some vitamin tablets."

"God bless your heart. Thank you Doctor."

"Don't mention, Ma Lu. I'll see you later."

Dr. Cooper went to Sinkor and told Mary the outcome of his talk with old lady Lu. And Mary was very happy to hear that her mother had changed her attitude toward Simpson.

The old lady sent for Mary for the first time since she was married to Simpson. Simpson had just left for work when the old lady sent to Mary's house. Mary drove her own car to call on Simpson at his working place, and tell him that the mother wanted to see her at home. Simpson asked to be excused from his working place and the two of them went to see the old lady.

"My children, please forgive me for what I have done to you. I don't know what to do to myself for this kind of situation," Lu said when Mary and Simpson arrived at her home.

"What is that, Ma?" asked Mary.

"I have neglected my duty as a mother; and I am too ashamed of myself. It was yesterday that Dr. Simatar Cooper told me that you are pregnant; the people have told us lies about your husband. Mr. Simpson. I don't know why I took for granted what the liars told me about Simpson. They said all kinds of things against him. I tried to do everything possible to discourage you from marrying him; and you went ahead and got married. At least I should have forgiven the two of you by now; it is almost one year and I have not seen you people. I am totally wrong, for which I must apologize to you and Simpson."

"Well, mother, it is fine with us since you have realized your own mistake. My husband and I have nothing against you. We are your children."

"That is true, Ma" Simpson said. "We do know that people in this little town talk about things which they cannot prove. They can say things without investigating whether what they are saying is true or not. They know more about you than yourself. They even know everyone's salary. I was surprised when a guy met me one day and asked me about my salary; he knew the exact amount Iam earning per month. At my working place, they call me 'proud man,' simply because I don't talk with everybody. But that was the way I was brought up. Not that I do not like people, but I would not talk with you if I don't know you. I have so much to occupy my mind at the working place that I don't stand in the corridor and talk about unnecessary things, as most of the people do at our working place. But I have no case against you personally; I look up to you as my mother."

"My children, please forgive me. I was totally wrong. Even though you got married secretly, I should have come to see you long before this. I hold your feet to forgive me."

"It is nothing, Ma. We have forgiven you," Simpson said.

"But my children, the doctor said that abortion is likely to occur, due to weak back and low blood. Where you come from with weak back, Mary? I never had any weak back in my life. As old as I am, I do my own work as if I am still young."

"I don't know what is wrong with my back, Ma. The doctor said that my back is very, very weak. I can feel pains in my back if I stand up for a long time or when I drive a car. This is why my husband does not want me to drive my car; he should drive all the time. Simpson will get some money by next month so I will go abroad for medical attention. Maybe I will go to Germany or the United States."

"Well, I hope that everything will be all right, Mary. We should thank God for your pregnancy. I hope to see my grandchild soon before I die."

"Ma, who told you that you will soon die? You always talk about death. You are not dying just now," Mary said.

"No, Mary. This time, we can't be sure when your time will come to die; people are dying very fast these days."

"We see you, Ma. Simpson will have to go back to work. He asked excuse from his working place to bring me here. I told you just now that I can't drive for my back."

"Okay, children, I'll see you either this evening or to-morrow. Maybe I will fix a nice rice bread for Simpson and bring it there to the house tomorrow evening," old lady Lu said.

The news of Mary's pregnancy spread in the neighborhood of Lucretia. Lu told nearly all her friends that Mary had belly, after several months of their marriage. She went to New Kru Town to tell old man Wesseh. The old man was also happy.

Some of Mary's friends went to her house in Sinkor to see her and verify whether she was pregnant or not. Mary would sit and spit all around, a sign of pregnancy. She refused to eat some food, including pusawa rice, oil, fresh meat and palm butter; she only ate dry rice with smoked fish and pepper.

Dr. Cooper announced the abortion of Mary Simpson to old lady Lucretia in three weeks' time. He recommended that Mary should leave Liberia as soon as possible for a thorough medical checkup.

Unfortunately, chronic malaria attacked Clinton Simpson. After two weeks of hospitalization, Simpson died. Mary Simpson decided not to get married soon; in fact she doubted whether she would ever marry again in her life.

Chapter 19

"Jack, you heard the news on the radio?" asked Dave.

"No. What happened? Who is fired from his job again? Or who died?"

"Nobody is fired. Clinton Simpson is dead."

"What! When he died?"

"He died at 3 p.m. this afternoon, according to the radio."

"What! That bitch had money! Was he seriously sick? Was he married? We did not see any woman with him; he was always by himself."

"Yes, he was married. How do you know that Simpson had money?"

"Nothing hides in Monrovia. We can get any news if we want to, and news is the cheapest thing in Monrovia. The people can mean you with their money, but they are willing to share the news anytime of the day or night."

"Even the man's private bank accounts you knew?"

"Yes. Nothing is wrong with that. Is it strange to you, to know someone's bank accounts?"

"It is strange to me, for accounts in the bank should be private. I would not care if anybody told me the bank accounts of say, Thomas Leanna; I have nothing to do with the money of people in the bank."

"To whom was he married?" inquired Libby.

"One Mary Tweh, a young and beautiful Kru girl."

"Damn! The girl is made, yah. Simpson left her all the cash."

"Yes. He had whole lot of money; he had a good job, too. Also, Simpson was a kind man. Someone will soon start enjoying his money from the widow. I think all of us will try our best to get next to Mary Simpson and enjoy some of the money Simpson left with her; after all, she did not work for that money."

"No. It is too soon to talk about dating the poor, young girl. The man just died today, and you are talking about someone enjoying his money?"

"What is wrong with eating his cash? He is dead and gone. These days we have to love these women in Monrovia for cash. Some of them are old and have lived their lives. Yet they want young boys, young blood to warm them up in the night. And the only way I, personally, will warm any widow, divorcee or old lady in Monrovia is when she turns the cash loose to me; I mean the raw cash. What else we want in life? Money. Even with your academic degrees, B.S., B.A., M.A. and what not, you still need money to survive. If you don't have money, nobody will listen to you, with all your degrees. You can work for stupid people, who have got the money," added Nat.

"Yes. These days, there seem to be more women than men, not only in Monrovia, but throughout the country. If a man goes to Bong Mines, Mano River, Cape Palmas, or Buchanan, he will get tired with young girls and women. Lamco, Yekepa is worse. Some of the girls and women who cannot find men are so frustrated. And we have got to help our women; they need our help," added Sam.

"Not Mary Tweh Simpson. That I know personally. She is very hard to get around. I attended the same high school she went to in Monrovia. Mary is a girl of principle. She is not a foolish girl. She would not yield herself to anybody because her husband is dead; if Mary does not like you, she will not befriend you," added Dortu.

"We will see if Mary will not get a boyfriend or husband within the next five or six months. For one thing, she is too young and beautiful to be wasting in town. Somebody must succeed. I think someone is planning his own strategy, how to get Mary in his corner, following the death announcement of her husband," noted Stanley.

"No, gentlemen, we should, at least sympathize with the girl. It could have been our sister who lost her husband. Why sit here and talk about how men will chase Mary and all those things? I don't think it is necessary," observed Nimely.

Such were the mixed feelings and comments of some boys and men when Radio Stations ELWA and ELBC announced the death of Clinton Simpson. Those who made these comments were presiding over club beer, gin, and whisky in a booth near the corner of a Monrovia Street. They were boozing heavily, but they knew what they were saying.

Clinton Simpson left a good-sized fortune for his widow. In all, he had about $189,000 in three banks in Monrovia. He had built himself a mansion in Sinkor; he left flashy cars, one for himself and one for his wife. Simpson was a well-to-do young man.

He earned his money by working hard, no crooked deeds. Mary had to compose herself because she was the only one to make all arrangements for his wake, funeral, and burial.

She bought about $3,000 worth of liquor and food for a two-day wake keeping; she killed two cows and seven goats.

She placed an order for a $1000 bronze casket.

Thousands of Monrovians and other people from Bong Mines, Buchanan, Yekepa, Bomi Hills, Mano River, and other places attended his wake and funeral.

Some people went to the wake to see the widow, Mary Tweh Simpson, and to see the mansion she was living in. Some went to the wake to socialize and capture new girl-friends during the two nights of wake keeping. Some went to the wake to sympathize with Mary. Some girls also went to the wake to meet new boys. Mary was too young for her husband to die.

Death, however, knows no age. It knocks on the door of old and young, poor and rich. And that was Simpson's call to go, never to come back.

Only the older folks sang the religious songs during the Friday and Saturday nights wake-keeping. The younger boys and girls drank liquor and cracked jokes.

A well-worded official gazette, read by his intimate friend, Magnus T. S. G. Tarpeh, reaffirmed that Clinton Simpson was a brilliant young man. He had headed several Engineering Consulting Firms in Ghana before he went to Liberia. He was the proprietor of the Sim-Ma Engineering and Consulting Firm in Monrovia that was the largest engineering firm on the West Coast of Africa.

Women shouted, fell down on the floor and cried when Tarpeh mentioned that Simpson was the only surviving child of his parents, who died in a motor accident in Ghana, some twenty years ago; that he was a source of inspiration to the poor, sick, and needy not only in Liberia, but in some fifteen African countries. Simpson made an annual contribution of no less than $20,000 to the blind and sick in African hospitals. A great humanitarian he was!

Even men cried when they listened to the gazette that Simpson left no child, only his widow.

Simpson was buried at the Palm Grove Cemetery that Sunday evening. A whole lot of people escorted his body to his resting place.

Theresa and Tommy as well as Tarpeh visited Mary every evening in Sinkor, to see how she was doing. Old lady Lucretia moved to Sinkor to comfort Mary; the old lady spent about one month with Mary in Sinkor. Ma Lu almost died when she first heard that Simpson had passed away.

One evening, Mary, Tommy, Theresa and old lady Lu were sitting down on the porch, watching the sun recede in the west. They were just talking about life, the meaning of death, the value of children and wealth and so forth.

One boy whom Mary knew casually came by to see her. He had not visited Mary before, at least not from the time she and Simpson had gotten married.

He said, "Hi, everybody. I am Wellington. How is everything going?"

"Fine," Mary replied. 'What can I do for you?"

"Nothing. I just came to pay you a visit."

"Pay me a visit?"

"Yes. You know that I live right behind you here."

"I know that you may live over there because you always pass here in the morning, either going to school or work; but you have not one day said hello to us, even if we were standing right here in the morning. I am therefore surprised that you came to visit me. However, have a seat."

'Thank you. You see, Mary, sometimes it is risky to be friendly with a married woman, especially in Monrovia. People may interpret your friendship wrongly. The husband may not like the idea. This is why I am afraid to talk to married women," Wellington said.

"What is on your mind, Wellington? Say what you have to say; don't beat around the bush. If you say that you don't like to befriend married women, you never one day saw Mr. Simpson right here, while you were passing going to work or school? Are you saying that because Mary has no husband now, you want to befriend her? If so, what kind of friendship do you have in mind?" Theresa asked.

"Yes. I saw Simpson here several times; and I did not speak to him, either. I did not know him; I did not know what he would have thought of me, with regards to his wife."

"Why you did not speak to him? Or was he a married woman?"

"No, Theresa. I did not speak to him, neither was he a married woman. But some men are highly jealous. If you try to be friendly with them, they only think that you want their wives. This is why I did not speak to him. I did not know him well."

"Do you know Mary well?" asked old lady Lu.

"No. But I want to know her now."

"Look, Wellington, I don't want any irresponsible attitude from anybody around here. I don't trouble anybody and I don't want anybody to trouble me. Since my husband died, I have not even seen you. I don't know you; and therefore I don't hold you responsible either, that you did not come to sympathize with me. But don't make me angry this evening. I don't want to be friendly with you; we are not socially compatible. I respect you as a human being, but I don't condone foolishness. Please get out of my yard very fast," Mary said in strong terms.

"Okay, let's forget it. I meant no harm. I see you people," Wellington said.

"We see you, Wellington. Never, you try this again with me. In the first place, if you want to visit me, you should inform me in advance. You can't just walk in on me as if we are friends. I don't know you well enough for you to march in my house. Tommy can call on me any time of the day or night because he is my friend. But not every Tom, Dick, or Harry can," Mary added.

"I am very, very sorry, Mary."

"You don't have to be sorry. We are just telling you not to repeat what you did today, or else you will regret it," old lady Lu raged.

Wellington left from the porch like a wet-tailed dog. Mary and her friends as well as old lady Lu did not give him an inch to support his grounds for the visit. Wellington had to apologize and leave very fast.

Wellington lacked the tactics for chasing girls, especially responsible women. Chasing women is an art; it takes quick, logical thinking, smart talk and good appearance

Theresa said, "But Mary, what kind of trouble is this? What was the mission of Wellington?"

"Don't ask me, Theresa. I don't even know him. He came here this evening before I knew his name. He is not the first, second or third person who has approached me like this. Some boys call me on the telephone here, telling me all kinds of foolishness. It is very annoying. Sometimes I have to drop the telephone in their ears. Some write, asking me to be their God Ma. And I tell them no. I need no God child. I don't even reply to them when they write me; replying means encouraging them to keep writing. I don't know why people have got no conscience. Is it woman they want?" Mary asked.

"Take it easy, my child. God will bring you another husband. God's time is the best," Ma Lu said.

"Ma, it is not the matter of God's time is the best. I know that if I want to get married, I can do so. But marriage is not even on my mind. The people are sick in the head. I am not hot for men. At least their manner of approach to me is very discouraging.

"Some meet me in the street and ask: 'Why are you not wearing black for your husband?' If you don't wear black, that means you are inviting us to come around you very fast.' I tell them that I do not believe in wearing black in order to mourn. I mourn in my heart, not on the flesh. Wearing a black dress, head-tie, and shoes means nothing to me. I tear them off if they are asking me foolish questions," Mary said.

"Yes. I was in the company of a group of boys, drinking just yesterday, on Carey Street," Tommy said. "Some wanted to bet that they would make love to you. They did not know the kind of relationship which exists between you and me. I simply laughed and told them to try their best. Some began to look in the telephone directory to get your number; and I gave them the telephone number offhand. They were surprised to know that I knew your telephone number by heart. I told them that you and I were working together; and this is how I knew your number," Tommy added.

"Well, I know the wounds in my heart, as a result of the death of my husband, would not heal just now. I used to love my husband. I still love him, as if he were living. He was a gentleman. He disrespected no one. No one, even now, can say anything evil against Simpson. Of course, people can say anything about him.

I cannot stop anybody from thinking what he wants. But if anyone will say any evil against my husband, that person will not be telling the truth. I do not hate the boys and men in Monrovia. But it will take a real man to take the place of Simpson, in my life. I know what Simpson and I passed through. I was close to him. So he was to me."